In loving memory of Edward How
and
To Charterhouse College
Magister vitae scientiaeque

CHAPTER I
POVERTY ' AND INJUSTICE IN THE WORLD
1.1 What does being poor mean in the globalization era?	7
1.2 Measuring poverty	9
1.3 Poverty in the world	16
1.4 How to overcome poverty	20

CHAPTER II
MICRO-CREDIT : A NEW TOOL TO FINANCE THE WORLD
2.1 What is microcredit	21
2.2 Yunus's microcredit	26
2.3 Muhammad Yunus , the father of microcredit	28
2.4 The origins of credit, from usury to the Monti di Pietà	32
2.5 The past Microcredit: "Monti di Pietà"	37

CHAPTER III
MICROCREDIT AS A TOOL
3.1 From a dream to reality : Grameen Bank	44
3.2 The structure	49
3.3 Grameen Bank against gender discrimination	53
3.4 The philosophy of loans without collateral	
3.4.1 Basic Loan	56
3.4.2 Flexible loan	59
3.4.3 High-Education Loan:	60
3.4.4 Loan House	61
3.4.5 Micro-entrerprise Loan	62
3.4.6 Struggling Loan	62
3.5 Grameen Bank : the bank of the poor twenty years later	63

CHAPTER IV

DISCLOSURE OF MICRO-CREDIT IN THE THIRD WORLD: OBJECTIVES, ACHIEVEMENTS AND OBSTACLES

4.1 Where Yunus's dream has flown to: diffusion, obstacles and goals 65

4.1.1 Microcredit and the United Nations   71

4.2 Microcredit in third world countries   75

4.3 Microcredit in Sri Lanka, Peru and Benin : three comparison cases 82

    4.3.1 The case of Sri Lanka   86

        4.3.1.1 The tsunami 2004   90

        4.3.1.2 Microcredit in Sri Lanka   91

    4.3.2 Microcredit in Latin America : the case of Peru 93

        4.3.2.1 Women and microcredit   99

    4.3.3 Microfinance in Africa: the case of Benin   101

4.4 Microcredit as a breaking point   113

4.5 The controversial issue of profit and cost   115

CHAPTER V

THE MICRO-CREDIT IN THE WEST : THE ALTERNATIVE TO MONOLITHIC BANKING SYSTEM

5.1 The Western financial system and the reasons for its stiffness   117

5.2 The alternative to the financial system: usury and its victims   129

5.3 The salvation of the poor in the dream of an Bangladeshi: microcredit lands in the West   132

    5.3.1 Consumer credit and differences with microcredit 139

5.4 Through ethical finance: the initiatives of the European Union
144
5.5 The characteristics of the microcredit in Europe 156

CHAPTER VI

MICRO-CREDIT ; MICRO FINANCE AND ETHICS IN ITALY

6.1 The banking system in Italy 159
6.2 Microcredit in Italy 163
6.3 Statistics of microcredit in Italy 167
6.4 The role of banks and institutions 168
    6.4.1 PerMicro 170
    6.4.2 Mag2 Finance 171
    6.4.3 Fondazione San Carlo 171
    6.4.4 Micro.Bo 173
    6.4.5 Compagnia San Paolo 173
    6.4.6 Fondazione Giordano dell' Amore 175
    6.4.7 Micro Progress Onlus 176
    6.4.8 Extrabanca 177
    4.6.9 Banca Etica 177
    6.4.10 Banca Prossima 180

Bibliography 183

Chapter 1

Poverty and injustice in the world

1.1 What does being poor mean in the globalization era?

The world is divided into two categories: high income and low income countries. However, not long ago, even high income countries had a large percentage of the population in a state of poverty. This does not mean that poverty has been eradicated in these countries, but according to studies geared towards measuring poverty, it has been reduced and even those classified as "poor" are less poor than others around the globe.

In order to measure poverty, we have to define it first. Usually poverty is hard to describe objectively, as it is a judgment made by the observer and standard measures vary among studies every time a different aspect of deprivation is analyzed. Therefore, we can start to define it with a quote from Mollie Orshansky (1969):

> *"Poverty, like beauty, lies in the eye of the beholder".*

Analyzing poverty can be described as an act of identifying situations that are unjust and unacceptable in a given society. Poverty therefore is based on a disparity in economic terms, which eventually degenerates into marginalization and, in some cases, delinquency. Poverty can push people to commit crimes, which if seen from a biological perspective, are just a manifestation of the person's survival instinct.

If a poor person is forced to steal because of desperation and hunger, it is a crime; if a hyena does the same thing to a carcass killed by a lion, it falls into the "survival category": the animal is just following the rules of nature.

Of course, this does not mean that I approve of stealing. Humankind has given itself some right rules to follow but it has not granted everyone the same conditions that make it possible for these rules to be followed. Because of this, the poor, in order to survive, have to bear exploitation by the more privileged.

Victor Hugo, in *Les Miserables*, exposes this aspect through his main character Jean Valjean, who is condemned to hard labor for stealing a piece of bread. This story is set in France in the years after the Restoration (1815) in which the social conditions represented are similar to those in some developing countries.

We cannot forget about Charles Dickens whose father was imprisoned in Marshalsea Prison, a prison located on the southern bank of the Thames in the area of Southwark and close to London Bridge, for not paying his debts. For over 500 years (1329–1843), this place hosted criminals condemned for subversion, mutiny, piracy and, above all, people who could not afford to pay back the loans they had received and who forced to stay there until the debt had been extinguished.

This prison was run by private individuals. The prisoners who could afford the fees had access to a bar, a restaurant and a shop and they could even leave the prison during the day. The ones who did not have these economic means were put into overcrowded rooms with dozens of other inmates who stayed there, for several years, even though the sum of money to repay was usually modest; this sum, however, was increased by the fees imposed by the prison.

The prison became famous for Charles Dickens, whose father was imprisoned for not paying back 40 pounds and 10 shillings. Because of this, he had to abandon school at the age of 12 and go to work in a factory. The writer based many of his stories on the life in these prisons, in particular *Little Dorrit*, in which the father of the protagonist is also imprisoned in Marshalsea.

What has changed since then? We are in the era of globalization, where faster communication has shrunk the world. Europe has managed to remove a large chunk of poverty and human rights are at the international level through the implementation of country-specific constitutions. This cannot be said for the rest of the world; some countries are experiencing the same conditions that more developed ones experienced 200 years ago.

1.2 Measuring poverty

When we imagine poverty, the first things that jump into our minds are the images of an undernourished African child, a squat or a homeless person sleeping in a train station of a metropolis. However, when we want to scientifically define poverty, the problem becomes more complex. This is because the concept of poverty is closely related to another concept: inequality. This concept is abstract and difficult to define since it is deeply rooted in philosophy and ethics. Because of this, poverty also becomes difficult to define.

This problem has led to the creation of numerous definitions, each one with a slightly different take on what poverty is. This does not mean that they are completely different; in fact, there are only three schools of thought on this topic.

The utilitarian one argues that a person is considered to be poor when they are lacking *something,* to at least a minimal degree. Economists that belong to this school of thought define this *something as* economic welfare intended both as a condition that gives physiological happiness to the beholder and as the total consumed goods from which he or she gains something.

The second view of poverty is based mostly on the concept of the possession of primary goods. The people who support this definition define poverty as a lack of items such as food or services, which are crucial for the individual's quality of life.

The third view of this aspect was born in the 1980s and Amartya Sen is one of its main exponents. Unlike the two previous definitions of poverty, this one was not specifically created to explain what it is. Sen's definition has a greater objective: it is a reaction to the paradigm of the utilitarian school in which utility is the only indicator of the condition of the person and therefore the only aspect considered when talking about social policies. Two typical assumptions of the utilitarian view are questioned. One of these is the concept that there is a direct and determined connection between the quantity of owned goods and the social utility that someone is able to gain from them. The other one is the conceptual identity of utility and well-being.

For the first aspect, the things that an individual can gain from the goods he owns is determined by many aspects and therefore predicting what someone will gain based only on the quantity of goods he owns could lead to a wrong conclusion. For example, the ability of food to solve malnutrition problems around the world can vary if we take into consideration different groups in a population, age, sex and environmental conditions. It is clear that the focus has to be shifted not onto the quantity of goods, but instead onto what individuals can obtain.

At the same time, taking individual utility as the only measure for the analysis of one's condition can lead to a systematic distortion of the degrees of deprivation. This is especially detrimental if people are compared among one other because of the different values that a person could have, thus affecting the utility given to the item.

This school of thought also criticizes the other definition based on the primary need of an individual to be precise. Two aspects of this definition, namely the lack of specific reference to individual freedoms and the fact that identifying the goods needed by a person to reach their best position does not take into account the conditions that affect them, are notable here.

Although it is the object of criticism, Sen himself argues that the problem can be overcome by interpreting more broadly the concept of "primary needs". For example, they could be interpreted as the basic tools through which a person can make decisions.

From the considerations stated above, Sen elaborated on a broader definition of well-being and poverty by focusing on the personal well-being of the individual and not on their specific actions, events and reactions as in the utilitarian definition.

In this case, the welfare of a person depends on the kind of life that he is able to have, which depends on what he is able to do and be. Poverty is the missed realization of these conditions. The outcome of this, of course, is affected by economic welfare as well as by who we are, what characteristics define us and in what context we live on all levels such as cultural, social, economic and familial.

Within this framework, the assets and resources available are, therefore, the means for the realization of their welfare, but they are not themselves well-being. To better explain this fundamental assumption, we can rely on an example described by Sen (1983): owning a bicycle is no guarantee of the fact that it can be used. A person may not have the capacity necessary to use it, for example because of a physical handicap. You can clearly see how having a good is not enough to assess the well-being of that person. The well-being, and symmetrically poverty, cannot be described in terms of "having"; they depend on what everyone can "do" and "be".

This theory, therefore, replaces the "something" of the general definition of poverty mentioned in the first paragraph, but not with the concept of utility or with a basket of basic goods, but rather with the abilities considered to be minimally acceptable.

The analysis of poverty is a theoretical problem of considerable importance given the ambiguous nature of the object of study: poverty may, in fact, be regarded relatively or absolutely and depending on your point of view adopted, it can be analyzed by using different models of investigation.

From here, two lines have been drawn in order to build a threshold below which a human being cannot survive in absolute or relative terms. Relative poverty is, therefore, a parameter that expresses the difficulty in the use of goods and services, referring to persons or particular geographical areas, in relation to the level of the average economic life of the nation or the environment.

This level is identified through consumption per capita or average income, namely the amount of money that every citizen can have on average each year. The conventional threshold adopted internationally considers a family of two adults to be "poor" when their total consumption is below the national average.

Relative poverty is different from the concept of absolute poverty, implying "the inability to acquire the goods and services needed to achieve a minimum acceptable standard of living in the context of belonging". The duality of the concept of poverty can be better understood by quoting a passage taken from Adam Smith's *The Wealth of Nations* (1776):

By necessaries I understand not only the commodities which are indispensably necessary for the support of life, but whatever the custom of country renders it indecent for creditable people, even the lowest order, to be without....Custom ...has rendered leather shoes a necessary of life in England. The poorest creditable person of either sex would be ashamed to appear in public without them.

Therefore, we can conclude that no single kind of poverty can be gauged (relatively or absolutely); there are many other faces to it. According to Paugam, three kinds of poverty exist in Europe:

Integrated Poverty: where an individual even if it is in need, preserves his position in the social hierarchy of his society. His integration in society does not constitute a problem. This is more common where large parts of the populations are in similar conditions.

Marginal Poverty: this refers both to the question of poverty in the traditional sense and to the one of exclusion. Those who are classified as poor or excluded are restricted to a fringe of the population, and, in some way, in the collective consciousness, they represent the misfits of society, those who have not been able to adapt to the pace of modernization and comply with the rules imposed by industrial development. Despite their marginal situation, it annoys many people because it shows the "losers of the system" and "delusions of progress".

Discredited Poverty: this defines those who are considered to be poor and excluded. They are rejected outside the sphere of production and become dependent on welfare institutions, namely the social system, while experiencing increasing difficulties. This type of poverty has a higher chance of developing into society usually defined as "post-industrial", a phenomenon partly related to the reorganization of the production system and to changes in international economic relations.

The different definitions of poverty make us aware of the complexity of this phenomenon: the poor are not the same everywhere and, therefore, the policies of the authorities to fight poverty must adapt to the particular

conditions of each country, region, province and municipality.

1.3 Poverty in the world

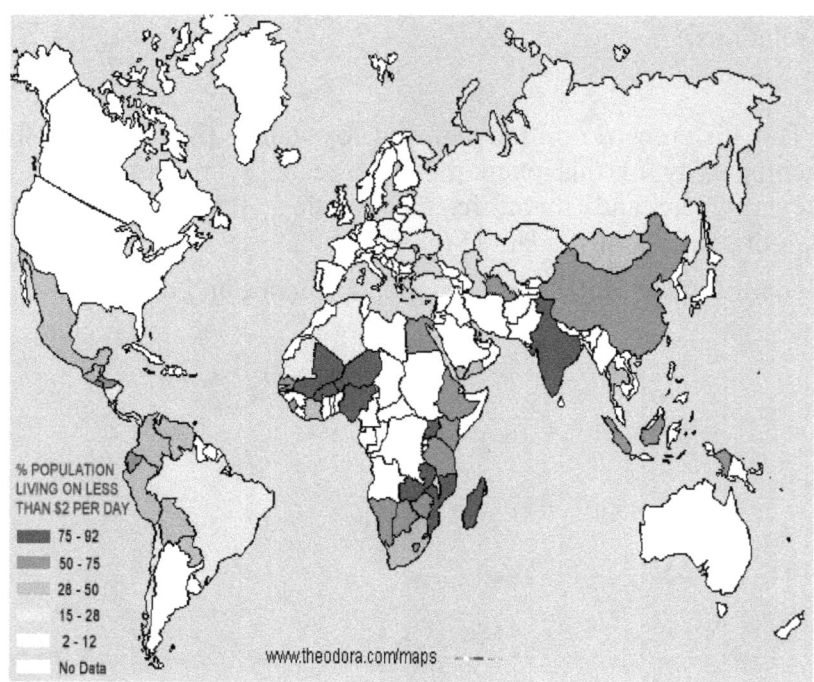

Until now, the majority of studies have been conducted by using measures of poverty based on consumption or income. However, some studies have explored other dimensions of poverty, such as the Human Development Report of the United Nations and the World Development Report 2000/01 on issues of poverty and development of the World Bank. According to data published by the World Bank, we seem to be heading for an overall reduction of poverty in the world.

In 2005, 1.4 billion people lived on less than $1.25 a day; however, the estimates for 2015 are surprising: it is expected that by that time the number of people living in extreme poverty will fall to 900 million. What is not emphasized is the fact that most people who manage to get out of that threshold will fall into the range immediately after: that of people living on less than $2 per day, which is still little.

Today, according to data from the World Bank

- About 24,000 people die every day from hunger and related causes. The data have improved compared with 35,000 ten years ago or 41,000 twenty years ago. Nevertheless, three-quarters of deaths involve children under five years of age.

- Today, 10% of children living in developing countries die before their fifth birthday. Even in this case, the data have improved compared with 28% fifty years ago.

- Famine and wars cause only 10% of hunger deaths, although these are the reasons that you hear about most often. The majority of hunger deaths are caused by chronic malnutrition. Families simply cannot get enough food. This in turn is due to extreme poverty.

- In addition to death, chronic malnutrition is due to impaired vision, a permanent state of fatigue that causes a low ability to concentrate and work, stunted growth and extreme susceptibility to disease. Extremely malnourished people fail to maintain even the basic vital functions.

- It is estimated that approximately 800 million people in the world suffer from hunger and malnutrition, about 100 times the number of people who actually die from it each year.

- Often, the poorest populations require minimum resources to be able to grow enough edible products and become self-sufficient. These resources can be good quality seeds, agricultural tools and appropriate access to water. Minimal improvements in farming techniques and food storage systems also provide extra help.
- Many experts in this field are convinced that the best way to alleviate hunger in the world is education. Educated people are more easily able to break the cycle of poverty that causes hunger. The question then is obvious: how can people be educated if they are missing even the most basic elements for survival?

What prevents someone born into extreme poverty from improving their condition? It is simplistic to say that there is no definitive answer. What is certain is that in a society until now driven by so-called rich countries, where globalization has eliminated the barriers between various territories, the "economic lens" is the best one to observe and analyze social phenomena. Even though cultures can differ from one another, in each of them (and at every social level), economic phenomena are driven by the same basic principles. Nowhere in the world will be offered for sale assets that have no market, because the seller would be forced to close his business. The same thing would happen if someone wanted to lend money: they would not if there had not been an implicit code of conduct able to induce the refund of the amount borrowed.

If we accept this point of view, it becomes clear that, even in the poorest countries of the world and among the most disadvantaged populations, the principles of economy, value, convenience and efficiency apply. Anyone can become part of the economic cycle, even without education; however, the means to become "entrepreneurs" are usually lacking.

Here is the key reasoning. Today, the best medium is money, a medium universally recognized. There are three ways to own it: to be born into a wealthy family, go to a bank or work. For a destitute, the only possibility is work, while the other two roads are closed. The first, because in obvious contrast to his condition, and the second because, in the absence of collateral, no bank would grant any loan. The only option left is work, the sweat of his brow, through which he sets aside just enough to provide for himself and his family.

Muhammad Yunus described this situation by highlighting the principle on which the entire banking system rests: "The more you have, the easier it is to have", and conversely, "If you have nothing, you do not get anything" (Yunus, 2010).

A part of the world's population lives below the poverty threshold because in some areas of the world employment does not guarantee the revenue needed to sustain a family. Often, workers are underpaid and exploited by their employers. In the event that additional liquidity becomes necessary, there remains only one alternative: not banks, which, as we have already said, do not give loans to those who do not offer guarantees, but usurers, who, with their exorbitant interest rates, drain even those minimal savings that the worker would be able to put aside for the realization of his project.

In the world, 94% of global income goes to 40% of the world's population, while the other 60% of the population is left with the remaining 6% of income. Poverty is also concentrated in certain regions of the world, such as Sub-Saharan Africa, South Asia and Latin America, termed "the global South". No surprise, then, that from one of these places was born an idea that could eradicate poverty or, at least, resize it greatly.

Muhammad Yunus, as discussed below, offered to those underpaid workers, the outcasts of society, the opportunity to redeem their condition (Yunus, 2010). The merit of this Bengali professor is that he invented modern microcredit.

1.4 How to overcome poverty

It would seem that poverty could be defeated easily, and it would just take 100 of the richest people in the world, according to Oxfam (the Oxford Committee for Famine Relief is a confederation of 17 NGOs that work with 3,000 partners in more than 100 countries to find the ultimate solution to poverty and injustice): A quarter of their annual salaries would void differences with the poor.

In January 2013, on the eve of the World Economic Forum, an independent international organization committed to improving the state of the world by engaging business, political, academic and other leaders of society to shape global, regional and industry agendas, Oxfam reported that great wealth accentuates inequality and prevents the global fight against poverty in the world. The dossier "The cost of inequality: how wealth and income extremes hurt us all" (18 January 2013) shows that the 240 billion dollars of net income of the 100 super-rich of the world constitutes a figure four times higher than the one that would serve to finally defeat poverty in the world. Oxfam called on world leaders to slow the increase in these incomes and commit to reducing global inequality, bringing it back at least to 1990 levels.

Over the past 20 years, the 1% of the richest people have seen their incomes increase by 60%. Not only that, the global financial crisis has accentuated this increase. The unsustainability of this situation is evidenced, for example, by the fact that 1% of the super-rich affects the environment 10,000 times more than that of an average US citizen.

Oxfam has called on world leaders to learn from the lesson of countries such as Brazil, where rapid development has not denied the principle of equality, or the example of the New Deal of Franklin D. Roosevelt, who favored the reduction of inequality and the contrast of acquired rights, by saying in 1936 that "For too many of us the conquest of political equality would not make sense in the face of continuing economic inequality" (Giovannini, 2013).

Chapter 2

2.1 Microcredit: a new way of financing the world

Before the 1970s, the way we used the word microcredit was completely different from the one today: there were other terms that expressed the concept of small loans. However, these forms of loans were hardly a fair trade, Usury in these cases was very common. (Pelgreffi, 2009),

Microcredit is now commonly identified as a useful tool to trigger independent development policies in the third world or in the degraded areas of some cities in the industrialized world. In general, however, in old industrialized countries such as the ones in Europe, it is still seen as a marginal phenomenon, a concept being tested in order to assess the impact on Western models (Borgoneo, 2012).

With the term "microcredit", you can define two types of financial assets: social microcredit and enterprise microcredit. The first term describes useful products and services that are used to fight poverty and social exclusion. They are interventions that aim, on the one hand, to offer concrete solutions to individuals and families who find themselves in a situation of economic difficulty, by granting a small loan. On the other hand, they aim to diffuse a culture of responsibility among the population by shifting the view of small loans from a grant to an actual loan (Borgoneo, 2012).

It is therefore not just temporary financial support to a person, but a social investment, which allows a significant improvement in their social and economic condition, helping in particular prevent future financial imbalances.

Social microcredit can be a first step to further development in terms of micro-enterprises or simply ordinary credit. In other words, once the phase of economic difficulty has been overcome, the loanee could be in a position to express and implement a professional project and generate an income in the form of self-employment or a micro-enterprise.

The term microcredit for a company is used instead to indicate useful products and services to promote the right to offer an economic initiative to the people. The goal is to create a virtuous cycle that allows micro-entrepreneurs to generate income and become economically independent.

For this objective to be reached, it is necessary to adopt a rigorous selection process designed to assess the reliability of the people asking for the loan and the validity and consistency of the technical, economic and financial aspects of the project for which funding is requested. Basically, what is being asked to the individual is a reliable personal guarantee in place of collateral. This approach to the question on the release of a loan is an innovation of great importance.

It is not the past of the people that counts or the profitability of the company (criteria that often significantly affect the behavior of ordinary banks), but rather the sustainability and effectiveness of the proposed project for funding. In both concepts of microcredit, the operators of the sector do not limit themselves to distribute small loans; their main objective is to develop, in potential and actual customers, the ability to activate their personal resources and planning (Niccoli & Priest, 2010). Microcredit puts the individual in the spotlight because the aim is to protect his condition.

Access to credit is a right that, if exercised, must be able to improve the social and economic condition of the borrower and not diminish his ordinary consumption and production (Becchetti, 2010). The definition of microcredit we are interested in is, therefore, the one that describes it as a tool of economic development that provides loans to people without access to traditional credit guarantees.

However, even this definition is not unique in terms of geography. In fact, it differs from country to country. The definition given by the Grameen Bank, a bank that, as discussed below, was founded in the 1970s by the inventor of microcredit, Muhammad Yunus in Bangladesh, the Nobel Prize winner for Peace in 2006, is:

Microcredit is a set of programmes that extend small loans to very poor people for self-employment projects that generated income, allowing them to care for themselves and their families. (Microcredit Summit (2-4 February 1997))

The European Commission has attempted to reformulate the definition of the Grameen Bank in order to make the concept fit well with the various forms of microcredit in Europe:

Microcredit is defined by the European Commission, as a loan under € 25,000 to support the development of self-employment and microenterprises. It has a double impact: an economic impact as it Allows the creation of income-generating activities and a social impact as it contributes to the social inclusion and to the financial Therefore inclusion of individuals. (European Microcredit Summit, 2004)

The variety of definitions of the term microcredit recalls another concept: microfinance. These two terms are not synonymous as you might think. Microcredit, we understand from the linguistic etymology of the word, is a small loan: an act by which small sums of money are given against interest payments. Microfinance is instead a much broader concept in which all those relationships of an economic nature that a financial institution can establish with a client are included. In particular, the term finance means all the complex movements of a subject's money, the handling of expenses and income of an activity and investment and the set of people who dedicate themselves to it (Stiglitz, 2006).

The prefix "micro" indicates only that the recipients are small businesses or individuals, however, in a very low income bracket and often without collateral requirements. It is not, therefore, only a small loan but also includes all other financial services such as cash management, receipts and payments, the use of credit cards and so on.

As you can see, these definitions – and in general all the definitions of microcredit – are rather vague and easily allow you to create different types of microcredit even if the common goal of all these definitions is to help poor people escape from their condition of extreme need (Borgoneo, 2012).

2.2 Yunus's microcredit

In recent years, the idea of microcredit founded by Professor Yunus has spread throughout the world as an alternative to normal credit, which continuously demands guarantees and safe loans; microcredit does not aim to enrich those who dispense it, but only free from poverty its clients (Yunus, 2006).

[...] Microcredit has been imputed to mean everything to everybody. No one now gets shocked if somebody uses the term "microcredit" to mean agricultural credit, or rural credit, or cooperative credit, or consumer credit, credit from the savings and loan associations, or from credit unions, or from money lenders. [...]. I think this is creating a lot of misunderstanding and confusion in the discussion about microcredit. We really do not know who is talking about what. (Yunus, 2010)

For a better understanding of the purpose of microcredit, we have to specify the difference between consumer credit and credit for investment. The former allows the beneficiary to gain access to consumer goods, which can either be be indispensable or luxuries. This type of debt most affects families throughout the Western world. Credit for investment instead means a loan in the short-, medium- or long-term to create income.

An important difference is that in consumer credit, the customer must already have a source of livelihood. This does not happen in the third world, where poor people often do not even have the basic elements needed for survival. Microcredit is thus a sort of credit for investment: the loans granted will act as a base from which people will start to climb over the threshold of poverty. Yunus's microcredit is not a charity, but rather an activity (by NGOs, associations and foundations) that renounces profit for the fight against poverty.

The weakness of charities, Yunus argues, is that they always need substantial funding from governments, donors and private volunteers; therefore, they are unlikely to regulate the flow of the incoming and outgoing money. Further, they are often not the same entity, nor are they constant over time. The money given for a particular cause that affects a part of the world rarely resolves the situation but only dampens it temporarily. Moreover, in times of major natural disasters, these flows cease with the interest of the international community or when the mass media stops covering the event. Further, the volatility of the benefactors, depending on their personal reasons, leads to abundant flows of money in a concentrated period of time and then to sudden decreases in the case of unfavorable economic conditions. This tendency and the inability to directly regulate supply constrain much of the action charities can do. Microcredit is not charity (Yunus, 2006).

The financial institutions that deal with microcredit are to all intents and purposes banks. They set interest on loans, obtain profits and invest in their own capital. The difference, however, to traditional banks is that microcredit banks look at the person and not his background. You could say they look at the being and not his possessions, as shown by Fromm. From this point of view, microcredit can find space in the world because poverty and social exclusion are present everywhere.

Yunus's main objective, the eradication of poverty, is based on the assumption that poverty is a condition from which you can escape. Referring to an old and famous Chinese proverb, "Give a man a fish, you feed him for a day. Teach a man to fish and you feed him for a lifetime". Yunus observes the futility of temporary solidarity and suggests a method of defeating poverty:

You need a dollar to earn a dollar, and the poor do not have access to that first dollar. Grameen will supply that first dollar to the very poor based on trust. (Yunus 2006)

2.3 Muhammad Yunus: the father of microcredit

Muhammad Yunus was born on 28th June 1940, a period when the Indian subcontinent was on the verge of gaining independence from Britain (the Indian subcontinent officially gained independence on 14th August 1947), in Chittagong, one of the main commercial ports of Bengal. The son of a goldsmith and the third of nine brothers (plus five dead children), he immediately showed his flair for International Economic Studies. He graduated in Economic Sciences at his local university and became a professor at the age of 21. He then undertook specialized courses in Colorado (University of Boulder) and Tennessee (Vanderbilt University), between 1965 and 1972 before returning to Bangladesh to teach at the University of Chittagong until 1976.

Yunus was always convinced that ignorance is one of the main chains of poverty and that the stimulus to revive the fortunes of the poor should start from university. The professor's reasoning derives from the observation of the conditions of disadvantaged people living in the villages that he crossed to go to college. This daily journey ended with the creation of the bank of the poor, the Grameen Bank (Yunus, 2006).

Bangladesh is characterized by a population density of 830 per km^2 and is constantly plagued by natural disasters. Life in Bangladesh is very difficult unless you are born into a wealthy family. Poverty and malnutrition are structural phenomena. More than 90% of the population is illiterate and 40% barely meet the minimum daily food needs. International aid sent to Bangladesh at the time of independence from Pakistan, reached in 1971 after a bloody war, has not led to any change mainly because of strong local political corruption and the fact that aid took the form of a "care package" and an investment.

As noted earlier, Yunus believes that welfare is one of the elements that fuels the vicious cycle of poverty. According to him, charity does not create development but only temporary relief, which does not encourage nor push those who receive it to rise from the state of poverty. On this basis, Yunus sought a tool that could be used to help the poorest part of humanity. Its aim was to revive the economic situation of the people and not temporarily dampen the gravity of the situation (Yunus, 2006).

The area covered by the survey of Yunus was the small village of Jobra, near Chittagong. Yunus wanted to was answer the following questions: how many families in the village owned arable land, how much surface area was available to each family, which were the main crops, which were the sources of income of landless families, who were the poorest people, who knew what to do and what prevented them from improving their condition, how many families earned enough from crops to ensure food for the whole year, how many were unable to achieve this and for how many months was it enough (Yunus, 2010).

The village of Jobra was divided into three parts: a Hindu, a Buddhist and a Muslim section. The professor and his students made use of an interpreter for every ethnicity and religion, making sure that the Muslim interpreter was a woman or a child. The analysis conducted by the professor pointed out that the cultivation of the land in the village of Jobra followed inefficient criteria that led to poor productivity.

The first objective of Yunus was therefore to teach farmers the rationalization of culture methods and to minimize waste. With the help of his students, he followed step by step the work of the farmers, offering advice and tips on more efficient irrigation systems and the downtime of the earth.

The results were rapid, and soon the crops were abundant. (The experiment was called the "Farm of the three parties". A third of the crop should have reached Professor Yunus. However, at the end of this experience, he recorded a loss because the farmers did not match the quantities set.) The experiment, however, suggested that not all possessed land should be cultivated and that the profits of high yields were only for the benefit of landowners: the workers, mostly women, were excluded, underpaid and without warranties for a callback for the next harvest.

Professor Yunus therefore decided to change the focus of his study onto this part of the population: the destitute, the poor among the poor. After all, the farmers, cultivating albeit badly and without any knowledge of agriculture, could secure a livelihood for themselves and their families, while for others, survival was a daily struggle (Yunus, 2006).

While the professor pondered how to take away the misery from the population of the village, he had a decisive encounter that led to the birth of his idea. One day, he met a widow named Sufia Khatun, one of the 55 million landless peasants. Sufia borrowed money to make and sell bamboo stools. Unfortunately, the applied interest rate nullified her gains. The same person who lent her the money then bought the stools at a price decided by the latter. Because of this, she barely earned more than 2 cents a day. Yunus realized that Sufia, in order to emancipate herself from the usurer, needed a loan of 20 cents to buy the bamboo to build the necessary stools.

It is well known that where there is misery, exploitation and usury thrive. It is hard for victims to escape this vicious circle because they are tied to this condition by the things they need in order to survive: if a person tried to escape it, he would lose his only source of revenue (Yunus, 2010).

No bank in the country, however, would give credit to these people, not even 20 cents if they had no warranties, not to mention the fact that the local moneylenders had the monopoly on small loans (Yunus, 2006). Therefore, the professor asked one of his students to complete a census of the people of the village who were victims, like Sufia, of local moneylenders. The survey brought to light that 42 people needed a loan of 856 taka, or $27, to escape the grip of the usurers.

What shocked the teacher was that only $27 would be enough for 42 families to be able to sell their handmade production at a price determined by them and not by loan sharks. Yunus lent them money, emphasizing, however, that this was a loan and that they would have to return it. From here, Yunus realized that the problem had to be solved by an institution. He decided to refer the matter to the director of a local bank and this is how it all started (Yunus, 2006, 2010).

2.4 The origins of credit, from usury to the Monti di Pieta

Although it all began in India with Yunus, it cannot be said that credit and microcredit practices were born with the Indian professor. The origins of credit are rooted in human history and, in most cases, associated with usury. Credits, loans and usury were united by the fact that someone lent money to a person and he effortlessly derived benefit.

It is well known that a loan is a financial transaction by which two parties agree to exchange money in different instances of time. Financial mathematics says that these two items are equivalent thanks to interest. It is the interest that in the past made the practice of borrowing "shameful". Since the days of the Bible, asking for interest on a loan was considered to be usury. There were no thresholds above which usury was considered and no one determined a "lawful" interest rate.

The prohibitions on the practice of usury date back to the Old Testament. The term usury appears in Exodus 22, 25 and Leviticus 25, 35-37. In both books, it is forbidden to lend money and ask for something more in return; in Deuteronomy 23, 19-26, this prohibition is extended to all goods (Barile, 2010, 3).

Even the early councils of the Church (the First Council of Nicea 325 AD, the Third Council of Carthage 398 AD) forbade usury, but only by the clergy since it produced a profit arising from a vile *immoral lucrum* (illicit affair). Later, in 806 with the Chapter of Nijmegen, the ban on lending was extended to laypersons.

Graziano, in his Decretum (1140), referring to a passage from San Ambrosio, bishop of Milan, described usury as anything that you receive more than the amount lent (*Quicquid fate accidit wear east*), whether it was of consumable goods, such as grain, oil, gold or money, or whether it was hardwearing as a plot of land or a house.

Goffredo da Trani (died in 1245), the leading commentator on the Decretum of Graziano, more accurately explained the etymology of the word 'usury', arguing that it was the price paid for the use of a thing (*usus rei*) or a required amount borrowed (*usus aeris*). Even Pope Urban III (1185–1187), referring to Luke 6, 35 ("*Et mutuum date nihil inde sperantes*") *in his decretal, the* "*Consuluit nos*"), remarked and strengthened the prohibition of usury, because the term *mutuum* appeared directly to indicate the temporary transfer of the ownership of a spontaneous and consumable good ("*quasi de meo tuum*").

In Roman law, *mutuum*, unlike *locatio*, was a contract that was free by definition. Whereas the use of consumable goods coincided with its destruction, the borrower undertook to return the equivalent of the thing borrowed. Then, to have more money or goods was considered to be usury. On this basis, canonists could say that "*solum in mortgage cadit usura*".

Usury was increasingly approached as a sin against the seventh commandment: "*usura east rapinam facere*". While the gain arising from "*turpe lucrum*" could be atoned for through donations and alms, the gain resulting from the violation of the seventh commandment forced a return of the goods. The councils in the XII–XIV soured the canonical condemnation of usury: the Third Lateran Council, chaired in 1179 by Alessandro III (1159–1181), handed out the excommunication and the prohibition of burial for those who lent at interest, while the Council of Vienne (1311), chaired by Clemente V (1305–1314), stated that a person who says that there is no sinfulness in usury had to be considered to be a heretic.

Guillaume of Auxerre (1160–1229), a highly influential theologian, justified the absolute prohibition of usury by explaining that it was a shame that, unlike murder, may never have a justification. By dealing in particular with credit sales, Guillaume developed another argument, brought up frequently to the modern age: the condemnation of the moneylender as a seller of time, which, as a common good, that belongs to all creatures (Barile, 2010, 10).

The Latin translations of the Nicomachean Ethics and Politics of Aristotle in the thirteenth century offered new ideas that enforce the prohibition of usury. According to Aristotle, currency is simply a medium of exchange from which you cannot get more money (*not nummus nummos parity*); rather, it is meant to be used as a measure of the value of the objects exchanged.

This conception of the coin as "sterile" was exposed by Tommaso d'Aquino (1225–1274). Along with Tommaso's reflection, Pietro di Giovanni Olivi (1247–1298) distinguished between *"sterile pecunia"* and capital, the latter capable of generating more money if given to capable men and industrious merchants. Through this distinction, Olivi paid attention to consumer loans, which, if banned altogether, they would have further impoverished those people in need of small loans.

Much later, in the middle of the fifteenth century, these ideas were taken up by Bernardino of Siena (1380–1444) and Antonino of Florence (1389–1459), who strove, in their writings and in their preaching, albeit with caution, without ever mentioning the source. Theologians and canonists worked out a series of *casus excepti* that, they admitted, under certain conditions, the loan should be repaid, as in the case of a request for compensation for losses incurred. Not all theologians and canonists had unanimously accepted these exceptions, however. Tommaso d'Aquino was reluctant to admit the "*damnum emergens*", but Azzone (died after 1229) coined the noun "interest" to distinguish between the losses incurred by usury.

The Councils of the Lateran III in 1215 and of Lyons in 1274 defined, moreover, the category of "*usurai Manifesti*", who, often in accordance with civil and religious authorities, lent money in exchange for a pledge in a public place: however, the accusation of usury fell on these people. Among these, the most notable were mostly Jewish moneylenders because of the biblical prohibitions related to the Jewish community. It was possible to lend money to Christians, or at least to all those not belonging to the Jewish community. Another significant point about the legality of the interest was that the loan was a public loan. The increase in public spending, especially on defense, prompted some cities to accumulate capital (*mons*) on which to draw in times of trouble (Fanfani, 2003, 125).

In 1343–1345, Florence consolidated the extraordinary taxation imposed on citizens (*prestanze*) by establishing a *monti comuni*, which guaranteed a minimum wage to the individual taxpayer. This event, considered by some to be a loan and by others a simple exchange, gave rise to a dispute between Francesco and Domenico da Empoli Strozzi (1353–1354).

This philosophy inspired the "*monti di pietà*", who specialized in loans for those in need. They were born in central Italy, but they spread quickly all over the Italian territory thanks to the preaching of the Frati Minori, such as San. Bernardino of Siena (1380–1444) and Bernardino da Feltre (1439–1494), who left one of the most significant sermons "De Monte pietatis" (Pavia, 1493).

The letter Inter multiplices of Pope Leone X (1515) put an end to disputes between supporters and detractors of *monti di pietà* and admitted the application of an *ultra sortem*, but only within the limits of the expenses necessary for its management. The letter Inter multiplices did not entirely stop the dispute on usury and on the lawfulness of the request for more than the borrowed capital: they continued until in the modern age.

The most famous controversy, in the mid-eighteenth century, involved the Dominican Daniee Concina (1687–1756) and the Marquis Scipione Maffei (1675–1755), which suggested to

Pope Benedict XIV the Vix pervenit (1st November 1745). Together with a series of official statements by the Church, this gradually eliminated extreme positions, until the Code of Canon Law of 1917, in which the usury was reduced to the request of a *lucrum immoderatum* (Barile, 2010, p. 22).

2.5 The past Microcredit: "Monti di Pietà"

The first form of microcredit history must be identified precisely with the "*Monti di Pietà*". These were born in Italy in the fifteenth century as charitable institutions, and they performed the function of guaranteeing access to credit for the poorest parts of the population. Small loans, as a rule, were secured by a pledge, without claim on interest or, if applied, only to cover the management expenses (Avallone, 2001; Meneghin, 1986).

The term "monte" in Italian (*mons* in Latin) is used to describe accumulation or mass, and the meaning was quite similar to that attributed to it today. The explicit clarification of the charitable purpose, selfless and Non-Profit del Monte was a key component that was so new and original it was qualified with such names as "Sacro" (holy), "della Pietà" (of pity), "Carità" (charity) and "del Soccorso" (relief). These names set it apart from the "pmontes profani".

The latter constituted a heterogeneous group of institutions, which made their appearance in the late Middle Ages and included, for example:
- Monti Comuni (also called "borrowings of state"), to which, usually, local communities recurred to [for example, between 1164 and 1178 Venice and Genoa in

37

1300] as a source of financing in certain situations in order to raise capital, paid with temporary or perpetual annuities, collected through contributions, voluntary or mandatory, called Loca Montium [This expression indicates that both the amount of paid-up capital is the amount of interest received], which could be (Muzzarelli, 2001):

-temporary (redimibiles);

-perpetual (irredimibiles)

-remain vacant with the death of the owner (vacabiles)

-be transmitted to the heirs (not vacabiles).

- Monti di famiglia and other established by private individuals (e.g., the "Mons domicellorum", "Mons Dotis", "Mons mortuorum") (Muzzarelli, 2001, 77).

These could be created on the initiative of noble families, brotherhoods, cliques or social groups to ensure an income or a capital to any third party beneficiaries in times of need, to undertake economic initiatives or on special occasions such as marriage or funerals (Meneghin 1986, 44).

Under this category, other institutions that provided forms of credit were grouped. Although different, they all had in common the "monte", a fund especially created for the aid of the poorest parts of the population. Under the same heading, therefore, are found institutions that differed only for the object of the loan that was not constituted by money, as in Monti pecuniari or nummari, but by a measure of seed or other natural fruits, as in the case of Monti frumentari, granitici, delle farine, delle castagne, etc. (wheat, granite, flour, chestnuts, etc.).

Creating "monti" to obtain social advantages, in the late Middle ages, was also common. In the case of "Montes Dotis", this was created by individuals or wealthy families to ensure individual income, to descendants or relatives, but it could also act as a form of public charity. Over the passage of time, the "Monti di Pietà" started to be formed by private donations or grants or public funds for the protection of particular personal circumstances [e.g. The establishment of dowries for poor children or orphans, in view of the marriage or becoming a nun].

The historiography of the "Monti di pietà e soccorso" shows that the long history of these institutions can be separated into at least three major historical periods. The first phase, the most studied one, starts in the second half of the fifteenth century. In this period, in fact, the Fifth Lateran Council (1512–1517) states the lawfulness of the "Monti di Pietà", both in the case of a loan free of interest and when they ask for it in order to pay for the management costs.

A second phase in the history of the Monti corresponds to the Modern Age and ends with the revolutionary Napoleonic era. In the sixteenth century, the number of Monti made by inheritances significantly increased in the Italian peninsula so that, in 1562, a census revealed that these entities amounted to two hundred in the Papal States.

There is, then, a final phase, corresponding to the entire Contemporary Ages, which embraced the revolutionary era to reach up to the present day. It starts with the crisis due to severe plunder suffered by the Monti, in much of Italy, at the hands of Napoleon's armies and is characterized, by the substantial secularization of the charity sector and the public administration of all the holy places subtracted from ecclesiastical control.

If the damage was not fatal, the change in economic conditions and general production and the affirmation in the area of credit of other public and private operators placed the "monti" before a dual fate: some slowly disappeared, others, the more solid, found a way to evolve in close connection with savings banks or agricultural banks, thus surviving until today.

The reasons for the birth and subsequent extraordinary diffusion of these institutions must be sought in the social and economic conditions in which they were called to work on. The Monti were born in order to combat poverty, to fight for morally correct distortions, especially in the local credit market. They tried to, in particular, save the people of the lower classes from the trap of usury that scourged mercilessly the weaker social groups of cities and communities, especially those who were forced to borrow small sums of money in order to deal with a temporary need and in a short time, due to high interest rates, had to return almost double the amount originally borrowed (Merusi, 1982).

We are certainly not in a situation different from the one that Professor Yunus found in his country. Both in the Italian sixteenth century and in the Indian twenty-first century, the phenomenon that hides behind poverty dates back to biblical ages: usury. The lawfulness of the loan at interest was accepted in late ancient Roman law, provided appropriate civil penalties such as the restitution of the sum in cases of unlawful usury, that is an interest greater than the maximum limits established by law.

Later, the law was oriented slowly towards the recognition of the fundamental illegitimacy of any form of usury due to the spread of a different ethical evaluation because of the Sacred Scriptures. Several, in fact, are the passages dedicated to usury from the Old Testament where, for example, in the Book of Exodus, we read that: "If you lend money to any of my people who are in need, do not charge interest as a money lender would". Other references are in Leviticus and Deuteronomy. On this basis, as already noted, the Church condemns usury.

The overall economic situation of the Italian peninsula in the late Middle Ages was characterized by a strong steady growth that, in the eleventh century, invested particularly in agricultural and handicraft, urging, in the course of the twelfth century, the development of a thriving "bourgeois" class dedicated to trade, financial intermediation or to finance itself in the new economy.

Here is how the figure of a merchant is born - the banker who possessed large amounts of capital lent it to local governments, European monarchs and popes, and therefore ultimately ended up as treasurer. The growth in demand for funding and the scarcity of money in circulation, according to an economic law is still valid, reverberated on the cost of money, producing a rise in interest rates on loans granted by the operators who possessed capital. These were the so-called "Caorsini" and "Lombardi" and in the first place, the Jews whose communities were widespread throughout Italy and practiced almost anywhere loans and imposed the toughest conditions, but their presence was often requested officially by the same municipal authorities that also discussed in detail the method of delivery, interest rates and the safeguards, translating into official agreements.

At the same time as the great economic transformations taking place since the eleventh century, the Church resumed with vigor the fight against usury, approving, through the papal decrees and conciliar canons, rules that are legally binding on all the Republica Christiana. The Second Lateran Council, held in 1139, condemned the "insatiabilem foeneratorum rapacitatem" with perpetual infamy and punishment for unrepentant usurers, the deprivation of burial. The Lateran Council of 1179, alleging wide dissemination of "crimen usurarum", forbade the sacrament of communion to loan sharks posters and reiterated, for those who are dead in sin, deprivation of Christian burial.

Usury practiced by the Jews was concerned, specifically, the Fourth Lateran Council of 1215, which provided for the cessation of all trade with them if, in the future, they had extorted "Leung et immoderatas usuras" to the Christians, in turn, threatened, in this case, by ecclesiastical censure (Merusi, 1982).

In addition to the role of the monti di pietà, institutions typical of the area and already active in the granting of credit to the marginal classes of society, there were also locally developed approaches to the problems of access to financial channels.

The tradition of Casse Peote follows the practice of tontines. They grew especially in the nineteenth century, and have still been active in recent decades, albeit in reduced form. This consisted as a form of association between people to provide the availability of cash loans on concessional terms. Beyond the purely economic aspects, run by a figure of reference (often linked to the ecclesiastical system), this structure of mutual assistance was based on informal knowledge, the relationship of empathy and the resulting reputational bond that is generated inside the group.

Chapter 3

3.1 From a dream to reality: the Grameen Bank

Yunus's believed in what he wanted to accomplish to the point of bearing all the risk. He initially helped 42 people by lending only $27 and recovered 100% of the loan. The dream he wanted to accomplish was beyond trying to free someone from misery. Within this action, he concealed the will to change the rules of the game, particularly those of banking systems and credit management. These were not suitable for the majority of Bangladeshis, who, in their current state, did not have the slightest chance of being able to access financial services of this kind. Yunus made all of this happen and he gave to a vast number of people the hope of reaching economic freedom by making access to credit a universal right.

Leaving the role of university professor was the last thing that Yunus expected to have to do, the last thing he would have wanted. Circumstances instead forced him to abandon his position, becoming first, inventor, then, implementer, and finally director of the first bank for microcredit, the Grameen Bank. This bank has a history characterized by many closed doors, a lot of work and a little luck. The mission created enemies, but, above all, many friends, who helped this bank establish its presence in Bangladesh first and then the rest of the world.

In Bangladesh, as in many other less developed countries, usury is a phenomenon deeply rooted and pervasive, as it was also in Western countries in past centuries, and even as it is even today. It is simplistic to say that those who live below the poverty line should stay away from the grip of moneylenders, arguing that it is a perverse system, made up of interest rates disproportionate to the sum paid, from which it is difficult to escape. In spite of everything, in certain cases, those who lack possessions have no other alternative but to become their victim.

For them, the opportunity to receive loans from a bank, which requires collateral, is inexistent (and it is, therefore, impossible to start a business because of a lack of capital) and, in the case of employees, wages are often so low that families need additional sums of money to sustain their livelihood.

Who is left to ask then if not the usurers, the only ones willing to make their capital available to the outcasts of the banking system? To many people, the high interest rates are a burden that they are willing to endure if the sum of money is needed for survival. That is why, even today, many people find themselves having to pay on the borrowed amounts, interest ranging from 10% a week to up to 10% per day, and having to ask for new loans to pay the interest of previous debts. Yunus was well aware of all this and, during his years teaching, he elaborated on an idea that would give people an alternative route to reach the financing they needed.

In 1976, just a year before the Grameen project became a reality, Yunus turned to the Jobra agency of the Government of Janata Bank, one of the most important in the country, with the intention of convincing them to lend money even to the poor people of the village. It is not difficult to imagine the reply of the director. The main reason for which such a request was rejected was the lack of guarantees that the poorest could provide. After several attempts, Yunus was able to obtain a credit line from the central office to the poor in Jobra, but only on condition that he acted as a guarantor for all loans.

Yunus had to sign each credit application and, with his collaborators, do all the paperwork, as the beneficiaries of loans were largely illiterate. In addition, obtaining new credit took two to six months, as each request had to be approved by the head of the office in Dhaka. This was a process so long and cumbersome, as is classic of all banking systems of the world, and in which in third world countries are no exception.

A series of fortunate coincidences, however, gave a positive spin to the project, which otherwise would have had a short life. Yunus met an acquaintance of his, at the time the CEO of Bangladesh Krishi Bank (the Agricultural Bank of Bangladesh), that shared with him his concerns about the general lack of interest of the intellectuals regarding the poor part of the population, the iniquity of banks and the decline in the country. Under these circumstances, it is no wonder if he found ingenious Yunus's intuition, and he promised full support for a future project with the bank. The director of Bangladesh Krishi Bank allowed Yunus to open the experimental agency of the Agricultural Bank, a subsidiary that would grant minimum amounts of funding to the poor, giving the professor ultimate freedom regarding how it should be run.

Suddenly, the project had found the institutional support of a bank and the capital it needed. The procedures were streamlined, Yunus did not have to personally guarantee the loans and the rate of return was 100%. The only problem was the number of customers, which was still low. It is difficult, in fact, to break down the wall of suspicion on the part of those who, from birth, were excluded and mistreated.

Moreover, the branch had little visibility, as it was operating only in the territory of Jobra.

In a meeting with several experts at a seminar organized by the Central Bank, Yunus was asked to relate their experiences. This took place in an atmosphere of total skepticism on the parts of the participants, who did not fully grasp the concept of microcredit. At that meeting, however, a senior official of the Central Bank was very interested by what Yunus explained and decided to support him. He called for the following month a meeting of all the heads of government banks, in front of which Yunus explained the project. These joined in the project, more to please their superiors than owing to real conviction. For the project to work, every national bank had to make available three agencies in the province of Tangail, near the capital Dhaka, plus a few others in the province of Chittagong.

The province of Tangail, on the opposite side of the country to Jobra, was chosen to test Yunus's project on November 1979. The various directors considered that the success of the initiative was justified by the fact that Yunus was a distinguished professor of the place and, as such, known and respected. In this remote province, however, his name would not have meant anything and therefore the results would be reliable. The turning point that marked the fate of the Grameen project took place in 1982, when Muhammad Yunus met Ama Muhith.

The two already knew each other. Muhith was the secretary of the Embassy of Pakistan in Washington when Yunus was studying in the United States, and together they worked to raise public awareness on the War of Liberation in Bangladesh. Over the years, Muhith had become a strong supporter of the Grameen project, and in 1982, he finally had the opportunity to speak at length with his promoter at a conference. As a "happy coincidence", as Yunus himself defines it, Muhith was appointed Minister of Finance a few days after their meeting. He played a central role in the months that followed, which marked the passage of the Grameen branch of a government bank to an independent bank.

Yunus's dream of making an independent bank found many opponents between the directors of banks and politicians. Many thought that although the project had secured excellent results, such a bank would not resist for long. Muhith finally presented the proposal directly to the president, who had taken office illegitimately following a coup and who, to gain consensus, signed the plan without hesitation.

Independence, however, was still far away. The plan of Yunus was to create a bank 100% owned by customers, but the Minister of Finance made him realize that his proposal would have an easier path if it sold a share of stock to the government. And so it was. However, instead of the quotas agreed, namely 40% in government and 60% distributed among customers (a formula that Yunus had already accepted without enthusiasm), he had to proceed by giving the government 60% of the shares. Under these conditions and with a little of bitterness, on October 2nd, 1983 the Grameen project turned, finally, into the Grameen Bank.

Slowly, things improved. In 1985, it was possible to gradually change the allocation of capital: 75% of the shares became the property of customers, while 25% was distributed between the state government and the two institutes. There were, then, further problems to solve. The first was the fact that the bank, although private, was run by an official appointed by the government. Yunus, although the general manager, remained, nevertheless, a government official who had to conform to its rules. His assignment in that role was also not final and it would only last "until further notice". Yunus strived to end this situation of precariousness. Keeping that regulation would, in fact, mean leaving full discretion to the government authorities, which, at any time and without explanation, could replace the general manager.

The Ministry of Finance initially opposed the proposal of breaking loose from the government because this choice would have meant the loss of control over the bank. Eventually, though, after the request was turned directly to the president and after several attempts by the Ministry of Finance, Parliament ratified the proposal. Under the new provision of law, a Director-General should be appointed not by the government but by the Board of Directors. Today, the Grameen Bank is 94% owned by its customers, while 6% of the shares are still held by the government.

3.2 The structure

The structure of the Grameen Bank is strongly hierarchical and it now has more than 25,000 employees and more than eight million customers. Customers are grouped into groups of five people, but they can expand up to 10 if the group wants to introduce new members (see Figure 2). Among these people id elected a Group Leader who is responsible for collecting money before the weekly Center Meeting and considering proposals for new loans from members of his group.

The centers are in turn formed by groups of eight to 10. Also at this level is elected a Center Leader from the customers of the bank, who chairs the Center Meeting, which takes place once a week, and decides which loan proposals must be submitted to the bank. The conference center has a dual role: on the one hand, it facilitates the collection of money, while, on the other, it crystallizes the Centre as a social element in which women come together to exchange ideas.

The role of the Center Leader is the highest that a customer can have (if we exclude the opportunity that every five years a person can join the Board of Directors). Often, the place where the Center Meeting is held consists only of some sheet metal that protects women in the case of rain. In fact, the Center Meeting is set on the same day of the week at the same time, regardless of the weather conditions.

Figure 2 - The structure of the Grameen Bank

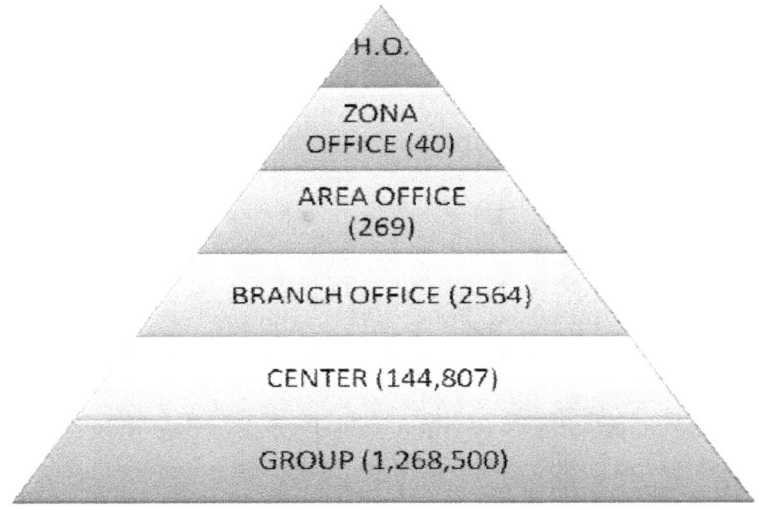

Source: Grameen Bank

In turn, the Centers are grouped by Branch. At the head of the Branch is the Branch Manager, who lives with his family in the same building or in an adjacent building. The Branch Office is a real bank branch: there are more than 2500 Branch Offices around Bangladesh. To help the Branch Office, a deputy manager acts as the treasurer of the Branch, and there are some Center Managers.

The number of the latter varies depending on how many centers are grouped in the Branch in question. Generally, a Center Manager supervises a dozen centers and must always be present at each Center Meeting. The Center Manager has the task of compiling the Center Meeting documents, collecting money, visiting the homes of members and taking note of new loan proposals.

The Branch Manager often attends the Center Meeting where major problems have been encountered, and goes to visit the homes of the people most in need. Center Meetings are always held in the morning. In the afternoon, the work is in the Branch Office. In fact, besides having to replace the money collected and control the accounts, at this time all the people who have made a request for a new loan come to the branch. The Branch Manager is the one who physically gives the individual the money requested. This activity is quite lengthy, as it has to follow a certain order. Women will be asked for their name, husband's name, signature and the purpose of the loan. The Branch Manager will finally deliver the money. In turn, the woman (or her husband) will count it within the Branch, otherwise future complaints regarding the amount given will not be taken into account.

The pyramidal structure continues as even the Branches are grouped into Area Offices. No customer goes into this type of office, however. The office area has an Area Manager with a deputy and assistants and secretaries who are involved in checking the incoming data from the various Branches, aggregating them for later evaluation and verifying the monetary magnitudes. This office is crucial from an organizational point of view, particularly for the management of information flows and monetary affairs.

In the Area Office, information arrives in hard copy from the Branch and here it is digitalized for the first time. The process takes place in an appropriate computerized area in which a half-dozen computers are assigned to employees that make use of a specialized software called Grameen Banker.

Refunds are taken directly from the Branch Manager in the form of banknotes. The Area Manager is the point of reference for all Branch Managers in the face of any problems. He, along with his associates, makes regular visits to the Branch to prevent the emergence of problems and monitor the performance of management.

Above the Area Offices are Zonal Offices. These offices play a coordinating role in the underlying layers and are in charge of spreading the few directives from above. The tip of the whole structure is the head office located in the suburb of Dhaka Mirpur. In addition to the head office of the Grameen Bank, in the same building are the offices of other companies such as the Grameen Phone, Grameen Trust, Grameen Fund and Grameen Health Care Service.

3.3 Structure of the Grameen Bank

It is interesting to note that from the outset, the bank focused on women in their roles as both collaborators and customers. Indeed, 97% of its customers are women. This decision was made for several reasons. The first is linked to the place of origin of the bank, Bangladesh, where the role of women is still very different to that in Western countries. In many Asian countries, for most of the Muslim faith, the normal rules of purdah apply. According to the Quranic vision, these lead to respect for the virtue and modesty of women, but in a more restrictive form in terms of their obligation to hide the sight of men, except in the immediate family. Many Eastern societies are decidedly biased in favor of men, while women are considered, for the most part, to be a commodity exchange, if not a burden, because they require a dowry at the time of marriage. The first reason why Yunus chose to involve women was, therefore, to balance gender discrimination: If someone in a family has to suffer hunger, it will surely be the woman (Yunus, 2010).

The second reason for which it was considered better to pay the money to the wives rather than the husbands was purely economic, since women are more careful, tend to build a better future for their children and show greater consistency in jobs. Money given to a woman will benefit the family more than if it passes through the hands of a man. On the other hand, the man has a different scale of values within which the priority should not be to the family: when a poor man has more money available than what is needed to survive, the family does not become the first priority (Yunus, 2010). In terms of the security of the investment, therefore, it is better to lend money to women than to men. The need to maintain the family, in fact, drives women to invest in the long-term to secure the revenue with which to meet the needs of the family in the future.

It was not easy to make women aware of their own potential, while very often men also hindered the process of starting up microcredit projects. Before microcredit became a popular concept among the population, communicating with the women of the villages required considerable effort. Yunus spent hours outside the houses, under all weather conditions, waiting for the women to talk to him, a stranger, and most importantly a man. As a result, there was help from their co-workers - who were welcomed at home more easily - after they had been educated on the content of the message to be disseminated to the "public" women.

The main reason why, initially, women did not accept the loans offered to them was the fact that, within the family, the man deals with the management of finances. At the beginning, moments of tension between husbands and wives were common. Even if you could convince a woman to accept the microloans, the husband intervened to assert his supremacy, asking that the loan were granted to him and not his wife. Today, the Grameen Bank lends money to their husbands, but only through their wives, who remain the main interlocutor.

When granted a loan for a house, the husband must sign a note that gives the wife the ownership of the land on which the new house will be built. In general, the Grameen Bank has contributed to improving the status of women in the countries where it operates. By entrusting the management of the loan to a woman or to a group of women, they have taken on a new role, the one of finance management, which has placed them at the center of family life.

However, they have also proved to know how to accomplish this task very well, obtaining a reimbursement rate that now stands at around 97%. There are rare cases in which groups of women, armed with this new awareness, were met by with resistance from their husbands, who prevented their wives from accepting a loan or beat them for it.

The employees of Grameen are mostly women. This has definitely been necessary for getting the message of the Grameen Bank across more easily to women in the villages, but also ensuring gender equity. Again, it was difficult to achieve the desired objective, as women are not normally allowed to travel great distances, those between one village and another, much less do it by bike, the only way to move easily in those territories. Now, working women in a still male-dominated society are no longer an isolated case (Yunus, 2010).

3.4 The philosophy of loans without collateral

To identify the poor to which to offer loans, Grameen found people described as assetless and landless. Different types of loans arose following the "revolution" of the Grameen generalized system.

3.4.1 Basic Loan

The loan principal is called a Basic Loan and this loan always starts the "career" of a member within the bank. If a person finds it difficult to repay the Basic Loan, it changes to a Flexible Loan, which allows her to repay the debt with peace of mind. Other types of loans include the Housing Loan, High Education Loan, Micro-Enterprise Loan and Struggling Loan. Figure 3 shows the mechanism of loans from the Grameen Bank.

Figure 3 - Mechanism of loans from the Grameen Bank

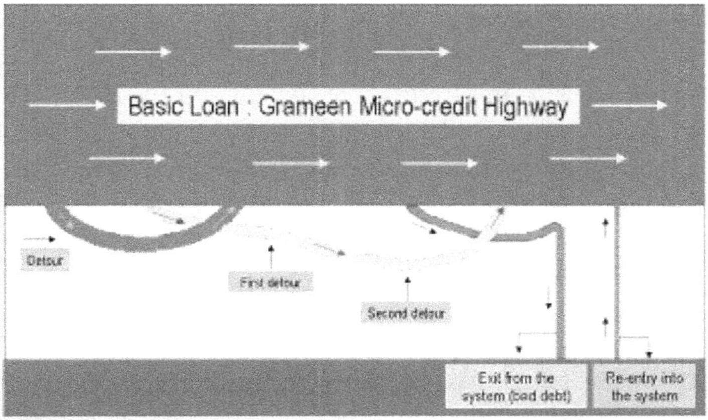

![Diagram showing Basic Loan: Grameen Micro-credit Highway with detours labeled "Detour", "First detour", "Second detour", and boxes for "Exit from the system (bad debt)" and "Re-entry into the system"]

Diagrammatic representation of the inter-link between basic loan and flexi-loan

www.grameen-info.org

The green part of Figure 3 represents the Basic Loan. This type of loan is definitely the main, as you can guess from the nickname that it was given: Grameen Microcredit Highway, the highway of microcredit. Grameen states that a person should always be stationed within the green area to make use of the Basic Loan. Thus, the customer can quickly and smoothly pay her debt and request new loans to increase her business and the conditions of her family.

In most cases, this is done in a natural way, but some customers find themselves in difficulties paying their debt and thus fail to meet the weekly installments of the standardized Basic Loan. In these cases, the client negotiates different payment methods, and then switches to the Flexible Loan, which will be described later. The loan can be paid off in full any time, and always at any time the customer can ask for a new one (not exceeding the amount paid in the previous six months), provided she has been properly paid in the past six months.

The Basic Loan has an interest rate discounted by 20%. Let us see how this is calculated by taking as an example a loan of 5,000 taka. Assuming that Grameen scheduling is based on 45 weeks, the installment that will support the client will be equal to 125 taka per week: 110 taka debt repayment plus 15 taka interest. In this way, the customer will pay 4950 taka to 675 taka debt plus interest. To overcome this problem, the last installment is increased by 50 taka to get a refund of the debt, equaling 175 taka. When the customer completes the payments, she can take out another Basic Loan, which varies in size depending on a few factors. If the customer has paid its debt without ever missing an installment or without ever having been absent from the Center Meeting, a future loan may be higher by 10% and 5% otherwise.

If the center of the customer has a repayment rate of 100% in the week in which she makes the proposal, the customer may be offered another increase of 10%. However, if this condition does not occur, but the client group has a rate of repayment of the loan of 100%, then the increase is reduced to 5%. Further, for each installment not paid the maximum amount drops by 2%.

For each day of absence at the Center Meeting, the maximum amount drops by 50 taka for every 1000 up to a maximum of 500 taka. If the interest is not paid within the specified time, the maximum amount drops by 2% for each week. In all five cases, the percentages are calculated on the amount paid by the customer in the past year.

The Basic Loan can have different durations depending on the amount of the loan and the expected repayment capacity of the customer: 3, 6 and 9 months are shorter than the standard is one year, and loans of 2 or 3 years are sometimes granted. For each period, there is a different interest rate, and then different weekly installments to be paid.

Moreover, the entire amount of the loan does not have to be retrieved on the first day but it can be withdrawn at the discretion of the customer. This method is convenient for those customers that have seasonal costs and when it would be pointless keeping all the cash amount of the loan from day one.

One of the innovations sponsored by the Grameen Bank is not to use "black lists", for which a customer is treated in an "unfriendly" manner. With this process, the customer is always available to the possibility of returning to take advantage of the conditions laid down in the Basic Loan.

3.4.2 Flexible Loan

The Flexible Loan comes into play when a client is no longer able to meet the deadlines set by the Basic Loan. When the bank is aware of the difficulties of the customer repaying the debt, it immediately intervenes to check the conditions of the investment. In the event of a lower than expected profit, which does not allow an easy repayment of the loan, a meeting is set up and the terms of the loan such as the duration and weekly installments are negotiated. This happens after 10 weeks during which the customer had not pay here installments, but is willing to renegotiate the debt.

Hence, the bank does not exclude the possibility of expanding its business: when the customer has paid properly for six consecutive months, and thus has found a better financial balance, she can still receive a loan equal to twice the amount paid in the previous six months, without waiting to finish repaying the entire previous loan. This shows that the bank's goal is to bring back to the Basic Loan all the people that went "down" to the Flexible Loan, without considering them late payers. The only limitation to those who have used the Flexible Loan is that the subsequent application for a Basic Loan may not exceed the sum of the Basic Loan that was turned into a Flexible one.

As shown in Figure 3, a Flexible Loan can have different locations. In the first case is a single renegotiation (detour) of the repayment methods after which the client is able to return to the Basic Loan. In the second case, despite a first negotiation, the client remains in difficulty, and that's why there is a second detour, giving them the chance to return to the Basic Loan. This cycle can be repeated several times until the customer fails to pay or is definitively considered to be in default (see Figure 3). Even in the event of default by a customer, she can return to be a member of the bank with the only condition that she must be six months on from being declared insolvent. Only after three years without payment is the loan considered to be unpaid.

3.4.3 High-Education Loan

The Grameen Bank also provides many types of scholarships for young students, aimed at mothers who want to give their children a college education. The customer must have an impeccable career in the Grameen Bank in order to claim the

High-Education Loan and at most two can be requested. In particular, she has to have never defaulted, never missed without authorization more than five meetings in the past year, and regularly deposited her savings in the past year.

The interesting aspect is that the student will repay the debt, starting one year after the end of his course, at an interest rate of 5%, as the remaining 7% will be paid by the Grameen Kallyan (which means welfare), an organization of Grameen. Obviously, to get the loan year after year, the student must achieve good results and can only attend certain courses approved by the Grameen Bank, such as Medicine, Engineering or Master's degrees in various colleges or universities. This type of loan cannot be accepted by the Branch Manager, but is analyzed by a board of five members headed by the Area Manager.

3.4.4 House Loan

The House Loan is given to a customer to fix or build a house. The ability to access this loan is granted only to members of the Grameen Bank for at least three years, with a good credit history. In fact, this is not a loan for investment, but a consumer loan, so the Grameen grants it only to those who can earn enough profit to pay the installments with interest for the House Loan. The bank grants consumer credit, although it is more risky, because thanks to these specific loans it allows customers to focus more on improving their homes. The Grameen Bank aims to improve the living conditions of its customers; therefore, the houses should be sturdily built and not made from mud or wood. The House Loan, because it is not expected to generate income, is offered at a lower rate than the Basic Loan: 8%.

3.4.5 Micro-Enterprise Loan

This type of loan is identical to the Basic Loan: same time, same interest rates. What changes is the amount for the Micro-Enterprise Loan must be above 100,000 taka. It can be said that it is a Basic Loan for the "rich". It was probably created by Grameen to see how many customers have built large businesses.

3.4.6 Struggling Loan

A "struggling member" (member who fights against poverty) means a person who before becoming a Grameen member through this particular loan was a beggar. Therefore, he had no family or friends to help him. The bank has also decided to give loans to these people in Bangladesh despite representing a class of "untouchables". The loan is at 0% interest; only the sum received has to be repaid. Since 2000, when this project started, 110,865 loans for a total amount of 140 million taka have been distributed. Of this amount, 107 million taka was returned and 18,480 customers have stopped begging and even 8842 have gone onto the normal credit programs of the Grameen Bank (Basic Loan). The loans are required to perform work such as the creation of umbrellas or screens, or to purchase goods to sell door to door.

In addition to all the social reasons that distinguish the creation of this type of loan, it is worth emphasizing that this bank aims to give access to traditional credit to many people who otherwise would have no escape from poverty. This scheme is actually creating future clients.

3.5 Grameen Bank: the bank of the poor twenty years later

Fifteen years after its creation, the Grameen Bank determined it was time for an overhaul of the system to make it more flexible and open to the new needs of its customers. In 1998, following one of the many disasters that have always plagued Bangladesh, the bank embarked on a restructuring process, which lasted until 2002, when Grameen II came into operation. There were three key changes.

The first was the creation of an emergency fund from which to draw in times of crisis. For this purpose, the Grameen Bank, which had become self-sufficient in 1995, did not ask for aid, but a loan from the Central Bank of Bangladesh, as well as the issuance of coupons to obtain funds from commercial banks.

The second innovation was a new supply of loans, which had greater flexibility, as discussed above. Compared with the only option that was in force since 1976, since 2002, the bank has offered four types of loans, with four types of interest rates:

The classical loan (described previously);

The house loan (interest of 8%);

The student loan (zero interest for the period of study and 5% after graduation);

The loan to beggars (fifteen US dollars of loans are interest-free and contractors are free to return the amounts they want, when they want it).

Finally, the last change was to establish a savings fund for retirement, a program of flexible loans and loan insurance.

Data from July 2010 indicate that the Grameen Bank now serves 8.29 million customers, 97% of whom are women. With 2,465 branches, it offers its services in 81,367 villages, 97% of the total number of villages in Bangladesh.

The work of the Grameen Bank has often been criticized by those who consider it to be a new form of usury that takes advantage of the unsuspecting population. Still, several official sources testify in favor of the positive impact that the bank has had on its customers. The World Bank, in a 1995 document entitled "Grameen Bank: Performance and Sustainability", estimated the costs and benefits of the initiative as well as the economic and financial viability of the credit system in order to analyze its sustainability and its potential in terms of expansion and repeatability. The high percentage of repayments and positive impact on wages in rural areas and on poverty reduction suggest that the benefits of the initiative have a solid foundation.

In addition, of the total amount lent to street vendors, more than 66% was returned, indicators of sustainability that are independent of whoever is put in charge. According to the document, the main merit of the Grameen Bank is being an entity that, through financial and social actions, has alleviated the poverty of the poor in the villages and has raised the status of women from a situation of extreme fragility. The Grameen Bank has also been thought to be "financially viable", an expression indicative of the fact that the profits earned outweigh the costs (most of which relate to loans and training).

At the time of the publication of the document in 1995, it was pointed out how the donations received by the bank would decrease at a constant rate from year to year and it was expected that the Grameen would no longer need them in 1998. Since 1995, however, a significant advance on forecasts, the Grameen Bank has not received funds or donations and is now entirely self-sufficient. At the time, the reimbursement rate was close to 90%, while today it has risen to 97%.

The credit program of Grameen Bank actually helps the poorest people use their own means of production to make the most of their resources and generate profits in a sustainable way. It also encourages the poor to save by allowing them to increase their personal assets.

Over time, steps have been taken to minimize the main cost component – the liabilities related to loans - by excluding from all services those who have the possibility of accessing credit at a cost lower than that required by the Grameen Bank. Self-selection schemes have reduced the default rate, and thus the costs. In addition, economies of scale related to several replicas of the project, in Bangladesh and other countries, have also contributed to the reduction of liabilities related to administrative costs.

Another way to reduce costs, the document suggested, would be to increase the amount lent per capita. This actually happens, but only after customers have proven to be strong enough to sustain previous loans. It is also true, however, that an excessive increase of the amount loaned is not feasible, as this would be contrary to the principles of Grameen, as well as the very concept of microcredit: this should fall under the jurisdiction of traditional banks. Evaluating the repeatability of the Grameen Bank in other countries is only possible once you understand the role that Yunus has had in the development of the project. We need to understand if this project found positive results due to the proximity of the Professor and his direct supervision.

If so, then the project would not be replicable; however, the facts have shown that it can be successfully exported provided that new branches comply with the basic principles of this instrument, that there is intensive staff training, a decentralization of decision-making and administrative flexibility.

Today, numerous projects have been launched in various parts of the world. What remains to be defined, and what should be analyzed for each specific case, is whether they have replicated all the features of the Grameen model. For example, some virtuous microcredit programs are based on individual loans without it being necessary to form a group.

In an international context, the role of commercial banks can be decisive, since they have the necessary organization to operate in the field of microcredit and can minimize the cost of set up and payback period. The problem is that these banks aim to maximize profit rather than social development. Their purpose is to promote growth and financial development through large loans, all of which are tied to collateral. To start a microcredit project, a commercial bank should allocate to this initiative a section of its organization, reviewing its structure and properly educating its employees.

The Grameen Bank has been able to export its model abroad in two ways. First, the bank has offered itself as the ideal model for those who want to start independent microcredit institutions in the country; it offers, to those interested, the opportunity to closely observe its work, so that the new initiative can become a "clone" of the Grameen Bank, but with another name. Second, the Grameen Bank has extended its presence beyond national borders by directly opening a branch in a foreign country, with the help of local partners. This happened in the US, in New York, and it will happen soon in Italy, given the agreement established between the Grameen Bank and Unicredit for the opening of an Italian office in Milan in the coming years.

Chapter 4

Diffusion of microcredit in the third world: objectives, achievements and obstacles

4.1 Where Yunus's dream has flown to: diffusion, obstacles and goals

The model of Professor Yunus has had unexpected success, to the point that his idea has been imported into other third world countries, many that have similar socio-economic characteristics to those of Bangladesh. In some cases, it gave excellent results, in others a little less, but what counts is that this idea has crossed geographical boundaries. It has found many obstacles; however, by traveling around the world, it has become a possible answer to the battle against poverty.

As already mentioned, in 1974, a severe famine struck Bangladesh, damaging the lives of millions of people. Among them, there was a professor of the Faculty of Economics in Chittagong, Muhammad Yunus. What struck Professor Yunus was that what was happening in his country, ravaged by chronic poverty, could not be remedied by the laws of the traditional economy.

Thus, after years of study in the field, the professor founded the Grameen Bank, which grants access to credit under conditions opposite to those required by regular lenders. The Grameen Bank lends small amounts of money only to people living in extreme poverty that cannot offer any warranty. According to the professor, it is possible to fight extreme poverty by granting small loans to those who have no access to the normal routes of credit.

Thus was born the idea of microcredit that is "flying" around the world. On this basis, other fundamental ideas of microcredit have been introduced: it should be provided without asking for any collateral, because the poor have hardly anything with a monetary value to offer as collateral. It must be intended primarily to benefit women, because in developing countries women with children constantly represent the population group most discriminated against in social, economic and legal terms. Microcredit aims to resize the male dominance typical of many traditional societies.

The loans are to be directed to women's groups and not to individuals because this creates social cohesion and solidarity within communities, especially at the village level, and sets up a virtuous circle of collective responsibility. In addition, the long-term experience of the Grameen Bank has proven that solidarity and responsibility for the group are an excellent guarantee of the repayment of loans. In fact, if a member of a group does not return the amount due, the debt falls on the whole community that has benefited from the loan and, in extreme cases, other loans are not issued to that group until the previous debt has been extinguished.

The loans, as has been said, must be modest and with interest rates constant over time. In this way, women facilitate the return of the sum and this also serves to increase their self-esteem, since they normally live on the margins of a society. The function of microcredit therefore is not purely economic, but also one of redemption, social promotion and the development of the entrepreneurship of women or groups of women in countries that are highly male-dominated and authoritarian. Access to this form of credit can often throw off the yoke of tradition that wants to relegate them to the role of mothers and wives: submissive, even economically, to their husbands.

To achieve all these goals, the model of the Grameen Bank requires that no women have to seek microcredit, but that microcredit has to find its own customers through agents that are appropriately trained and sent into the field. This implies a direct, transparent and continuous link between the officials of the bank or association that provides loans and those chosen to start business projects. This relationship, based on trust and personal knowledge of the customer, is the basis of a type of credit called proximity credit.

Naturally, this system has limitations. The largest of these limits is that microcredit is not a magic formula, although it has been an undeniable revolution and represents a break with the traditional systems of credit, which were exclusive, typical of the capitalist model rather than the single "medicine" for the ills of the world (Yunus, 2006).

Some economic experts, while recognizing the merit of microcredit in providing an immediate solution to crisis situations surrounding poor people, dispute that it overemphasizes the weight of this micro-economy, losing sight of the real value of this change. In fact, they argue that the development of a country is not driven by the sum of the individual micro reality, which does not create development, but simply self-supporting schemes, but rather by medium-sized businesses, the real engine of economies, that in developing countries are almost totally absent.

There is therefore, according to these economists, a middle ground between the "fruit stand" and "large corporation", so that the economic mechanism remains incomplete between two extremes: the micro-enterprise and individual capitalism of corporations. This absence has been dubbed "the missing middle" (Surowiecki, 2008). However, in spite of what economists say, freeing just one family from extreme poverty is a success. It may seem like a drop in the ocean, but it is also true that the sea is made of many drops.

4.1.1 Microcredit and the United Nations

In 1998, the UN warned that microcredit alone cannot eradicate poverty in the world. In 1998, the UN General Assembly during the 53rd session adopted resolution 53/198, proclaiming 2005 the International Year of Microcredit, recognizing and reaffirming the nature of the instrument is not unrealistic for the fight against poverty. At the "Microcredit Summit" held in 1997 in Washington, DC, 51 donors agreed to a project that, by 2005, would allow 100 million poor families to benefit from microcredit programs. The summit organizers expected that reaching this goal would require additional outlays of $26 billion.

In the resolution, there is the invitation to promote and develop microcredit programs in the world and in particular its call to governments, UN bodies and NGOs working in the field to spread the role that such an instrument has in eradicating poverty and improving social development.

According to its resolution 58/221, the same General Assembly of the United Nations approved the Plan of Action that has five key objectives:
1. To help achieve the "Millennium Development Goals";

2. To increase public awareness of the role of microcredit in the eradication of poverty;

3. To identify the most significant measures to stimulate the sustainable development of financial instruments in favor of the lower classes;

4. To increase the capacity and efficiency of the service providers of microcredit and microfinance in responding to the needs of the poorer classes;

5. To encourage innovation and partnerships

Through resolution 58/488, the General Assembly asked member states to establish National Committees to prepare and coordinate the initiatives for the year. We also read in the UN report that informal agreements relating to small loans have a long history and have had success, especially in rural areas. Examples of such traditional forms of microfinance can still be found in Kenya ("merry-go-rounds"), Ghana (susu), Nigeria (esusu) and Malawi (chiperegani). These agreements are not only effective in the absence of formal bank loans; in some cases, they are preferable.

Participants earn credibility and a certain level of protection against economic fluctuations or family difficulties thanks to a social system of mutual support; guarantees are provided jointly. The practice of providing, through national and international agencies, small loans on a large scale as a means of combating poverty has been well established, especially in an era of reduced expectations to the public sector. When government spending decreases, microcredit offers hope to release the entrepreneurial potential of the poor, especially the poorest women, at moderate cost and with minimum bureaucracy.

Since the beginning of the decade, approximately 3,000 microfinance institutions have been created in countries in the developing world. According to the report of the Secretary-General (A/53/223), it is clear that "there are limits to the use of credit as a tool for the eradication of poverty, since many people, especially the poorest among the poor lack entrepreneurial skills and partly because they are devoid of stimuli". In addition, despite the proliferation of a vast literature on the subject, the various protests for higher reimbursement rates or for continuous improvements in the standards of living of the beneficiaries are not supported with sufficient conviction. The report also warns not to move the scarce funds for development assistance from key sectors such as agriculture, infrastructure, health, sanitation and education.

The report, prepared by the Division for Social Policy and Development of the Department of Economic and Social Affairs, lists some of the difficulties that have been encountered by existing institutions. In many developing countries, interest rates are on the whole relatively high, and with a heavy risk premium, meaning that the interest rates for microfinance can become very high. Administrative structures are normally either fragile or rudimentary, and sometimes cause high transaction costs. The report argues that with transaction costs, which are added on top of high interest rates, it is uncertain whether it would be economically convenient to still require a margin 30% to 50%.

A recent alternative approach to microfinance favors the granting of loans to anyone who is in a position to repay the loan, regardless of the presentation of a plan for a small business in the market or in the informal sector. The report, however, shows that this there is the inherent risk that beneficiaries consume their loan rather than investing it.

To maximize the undoubted success of many microcredit programs, the report recommends strengthening the administrative structure, suggests that these loans should also be granted in the context of gaining access to land and in the presence of appropriate technologies, markets and groups of mutual support and advice, and asks that microfinance should be seen as one component of an overall strategy to support small commercial yields.

The report indicates that in order to ensure long-term sustainability in microcredit operations, a service for savings, such as a credit union connected to the microfinance institution, should be implemented. Without a perspective of long-term sustainability, the establishment of microcredit immediately becomes in danger of collapsing or becoming a subtle and devious charitable organization.

The report of the Secretary-General welcomes the establishment by the World Bank (which has a portfolio of $218 million for microcredit) of a Consultative Group to Assist the Poorest (CGAP) aimed at coordinating international efforts in the field of microfinance, collect reliable information and promote best practice. The report argues that "the process of CGAP should be strengthened" and that "the United Nations system needs also to spread a more realistic understanding of the potential approaches to micro-credit, and to incorporate these approaches in the broader perspective in the struggle for the eradication of poverty" (UN, 2013).

4.2 Microcredit in third world countries

Data on the prevalence of microcredit are available today in the 2013 Report "Microcredit Summit Campaign" (Microcredit Summit Campaign is a project of RESULTS Educational Fund, a US organization committed to combat hunger and poverty in the world). This report is the result of research conducted on behalf of the UN on the activities of various microfinance institutions that provided, in 2011, the results achieved by them in 2010.

If one considers the geographical distribution of the institutions, you can see from Figure 5 that the highest percentages are found in developing countries (1009 Sub-Saharan Africa, 1746 in Asia and the Pacific, 647 in Latin America and the Caribbean, 91 in the Middle East and North Africa), while the remaining 159 are located in industrialized countries (86 in North America and Western Europe, 73 in Eastern Europe and Central Asia).

Figure 4 - Results of the Verification Process, 12/31/99–12/31/10

Date	Number of Institutions Verified	Number of Poorest Clients Verified	Percent Verified of Total Poorest Clients Reported	Total Number of Poorest Clients Reported
12/31/99	78	9,274,385	67	13,779,872
12/31/00	138	12,752,645	66	19,327,451
12/31/01	211	21,771,448	81	26,878,332
12/31/02	234	35,837,356	86	41,594,778
12/31/03	286	47,458,191	87	54,785,433
12/31/04	330	58,450,926	88	66,614,871
12/31/05	420	64,062,221	78	81,949,036
12/31/06	327	79,181,635	85	92,922,574
12/31/07	284	84,916,899	80	106,584,679
12/31/09*	327	119,490,847	93	128,220,051
12/31/10	**328**	**72,385,972**	**53**	**137,547,441**

Source: Microcredit Summit Campaign 2013

In 2009, for the first time in a decade, the campaign did not collect or verify data nor did it release a State of the Microcredit Summit Campaign Report, which is why there are no December 31, 2008 figures.

The continued growth of microcredit, due to the recent global economic crisis, is approaching the goal that the UN has set for 2015. The intention of the United Nations is to reach 175 million beneficiaries, most under the poverty line, living on less than a dollar a day. Considering that in 2010 the recipients of micro-loans amounted to about 138 million, there is a strong belief that it can successfully achieve this goal.

Figure 5 - Regional Breakdown of Microfinance Data

Region	Number of programs reporting	Number of total clients in 2009	Number of total clients in 2010	Number of poorest clients in 2009	Number of poorest clients in 2010	Number of poorest women clients in 2009	Number of poorest women clients in 2010
Sub-Saharan Africa	1,009	10,776,726	12,692,579	6,360,861	7,248,732	3,935,808	4,783,256
Asia & the Pacific	1,746	156,403,658	169,125,878	117,178,142	125,530,437	97,385,541	104,752,430
Latin America & the Caribbean	647	12,257,181	13,847,987	2,834,742	2,919,646	1,935,685	2,363,100
Middle East & North Africa	91	4,552,387	4,290,735	1,492,322	1,680,181	1,217,113	1,165,358
Developing World Totals	3,493	183,989,952	199,957,179	127,866,067	137,378,996	104,474,146	113,064,144
North America & Western Europe	86	148,628	155,254	109,318	41,809	56,651	12,214
Eastern Europe & Central Asia	73	5,996,500	5,202,069	233,810	126,636	163,318	62,294
Industrialized World Totals	159	6,145,128	5,357,323	343,128	168,445	219,969	74,508
Global Totals	3,652	190,135,080	205,314,502	128,209,195	137,547,441	104,694,115	113,138,652

Source: Microcredit Summit Campaign 2013

Figure 6 - Regional Breakdown of Access to Microfinance

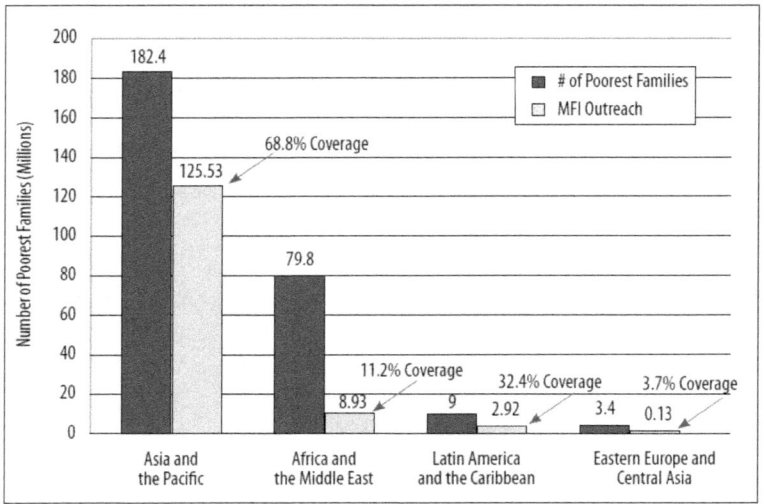

Source: Microcredit Summit Campaign 2013

Figure 7 - Growth in the Number of Poorest Women Reached in Relation to Total Poorest People Reached

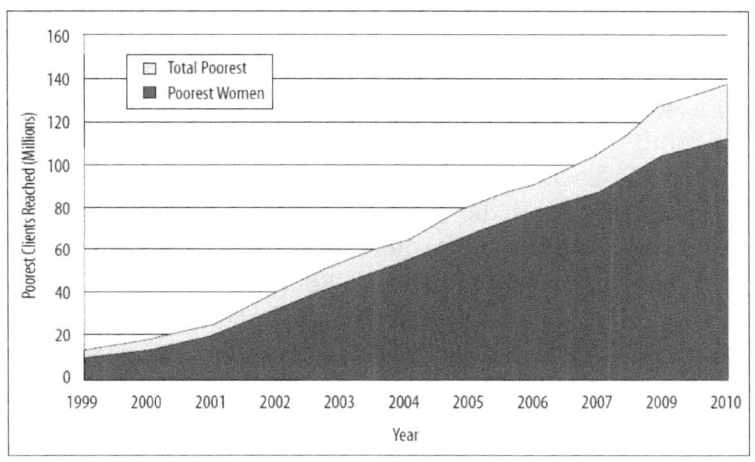

Source: Source: Microcredit Summit Campaign 2013

In the Asian region, microcredit has had the most extensive development. An innovative approach to reduce risk, which has been used successfully by the distribution system of the Grameen Bank, is peer-group monitoring. Some studies, however, have suggested that the high rates of repayment of Grameen are also partially attributable to the conduct of public meetings (to which participation is mandatory) for the repayment of loan installments and the collection of savings (UN, 2013). It is noted that these meetings reinforce a culture of discipline, a practice towards redemptions and a sense of responsibility among staff. Not all microfinance institutions use "peer groups". Other institutions, such as Bank Rakyat Indonesia, which serves 2.5 million customers and 12 million small investors, rely on the reputation of the clients and financial agents recruited locally rather than the presence of collateral.

The Bank of Agriculture and Agricultural Cooperatives of Thailand serves approximately 1 million small entrepreneurs and 3.6 million small investors. Newcomers, such as the Association for Social Development in Bangladesh, with half a million customers, and the People's Credit Fund in Vietnam, with more than 200,000 customers, are other examples of the growth potential of the industry. Other institutions such as ACLEDA in Cambodia, the Buro-Tangail and SEWA Bank of India and the AIMS Ikhtiar of Malaysia also seem to have achieved good results.

Various institutions in Asia are involved in the provision of microfinance services. They include commercial banks, rural banks, cooperatives, credit unions and NGOs. Their methods of action range from Grameen-style systems of solidarity groups to institutions that deal directly with individuals in a group system. Reports indicate that some institutions have gone beyond credit, offering other financial services and insurance. Both the Grameen Bank and the Committee for Rural Development in Bangladesh offer non-financial services, such as facilities for the distribution of its customers' products to retailers.

In Latin America, the initiative of an American tennis player, Joseph Blatchford, stands out, who created Accion, an NGO whose mission is to help the poorest through mutual support. It started to install power lines and build schools and community centers, and Accion then decided to support micro-enterprises. Its reimbursement rate is close to 100% and 77% of its customers are women.

In 1992, BancoSol became, along with many diversified products, the bank of reference in the world of microfinance in Latin America. Accion Internacional and its affiliates have provided over the past five years $1 billion in loans to small-scale entrepreneurs. The first part of the loans is between 100 and 200 dollars, and the overall repayment rate is around 98%. Its network of nineteen subsidiaries in Latin America and North America provides $300 million a year in loans to poor entrepreneurs (56% of whom are women). Since 1987, the Accion network has grown from 13,000 customers to more than 285,000. The six largest affiliates now provide $1 million per month in loans.

BancoSol in Bolivia, which has developed from an NGO for the provision of credit to a fully-fledged commercial bank, provides financial services to 67,000 people, more than half of the total customers of the entire Bolivian banking system. ADEMI in the Dominican Republic and ACP in Peru seem to have achieved sustainability, too.

Peru, for example, is one of the countries that are most careful about microcredit. This is characterized by the formalization of the sector in response to a logic that aims at the synthesis between social components and banking components through a particularly complex process, which is subject to constant checks to confirm the validity of the solution. This trend manifests itself in the history of Mibanco, which represents a particularly interesting case, as it grew from the transformation of an NGO (ACP) in a commercial bank that maintains the mission of serving the poor part of the population (UN, 2013).

In Latin American, microcredit has evolved into a banking structure that is similar to the Grameen Bank. It is in a consolidated phase of microcredit where NGOs have been created to support those who live in extreme poverty and have become structures attentive to the costs and profits.

This step, however, is polluting the true objective of the idea of Professor Yunus, because when something defined as non-profit becomes a commercial organization, focused on profits and costs, it can create more and more barriers, which become increasingly difficult to overcome for the extreme poor. This does not mean that in Latin America microcredit does not work, but it is losing the initial idea developed by Yunus.

In West Africa, where microfinance institutions are still in their infancy, a study by the World Bank of nine microfinance schemes (the Pride, Crédit Rural, and Crédit Mutuel de Guinee Guinea; Crédit Mutuel of Senegal, and Village Banks Nganda in Senegal; Réseau des Caisses Populaires and Sahel Action PPPCR in Burkina Faso and Caisses Villageoises du Pays Dogon in Mali and Kafo Jiginew) shows how all these programs strictly follow the best practices in the field of microfinance.

The study gives a good evaluation of these programs, in terms of the sustainability of the loan for small business owners. All nine programs are located close to their customers and in the most important areas of the country. Further, they utilize technologies for the loan that are simple, appropriate to the cultural environment and cost-effective for both the creditor and the borrower. By using these techniques, which are effective at achieving high repayment rates, most organizations now provide savings programs that meet the basic needs of many people (UN, 2013).

The emergence of microcredit has prompted some institutions that operate in such contexts to make use of appropriate credit scoring systems to assess the reliability of an applicant for microcredit. Among them, we can mention: "BancoSol" in Bolivia, "African Bank / Credit Indemnity" and "Teba Bank" in South Africa, "Mibanco" in Peru, "United Bulgarian Bank" in Bulgaria and "Unibanka" in Latvia. Each has developed a precise scoring model for the specific products offered based on the data available. Nevertheless, credit scoring in the microfinance sector is still not widespread and it is uncertain whether it will find fertile ground in the future, even though microcredit is a loan in all respects.

This stems from the different contexts in which such an instrument has been developed, from its objectives, mainly social, and from its assessments of requests, in most cases subjective for micro. In addition, because applicants do not have access to banking and financial circuits owing to the lack of the necessary requirements, it is quite a task to quantify their solvency.

The statistical models implemented for the prediction of "creditworthiness" in the context of consumer credit, such as logistic regressions, help analysts estimate the probability of a return on the loan. The dependent variable of the models built, then, is binary and, in general, takes a value equal to 1 if the client is considered to be a "good payer" and equal to 0 if the customer is a "bad payer". The terms "good payer" and "bad payer" are not, however, appropriate for classifying a beneficiary of microcredit. This is because the relationship established between the applicant and the institution providing the loan is based on trust.

Because of the lack of information on the individual, the solvency of the applicant cannot be quantified numerically; therefore, the institution evaluates the request by using the limited data available and trusting their instincts. If the request, taking charge from any Evaluation Committee, is considered to be sustainable by microcredit standards, the loan is disbursed and, with it, the confidence in the good morals of the beneficiary. The utility company, in fact, hopes and believes that microcredit helps the recipient overcome the state of crisis in which she is located if recognized as an instrument with a powerful social value. What the institution shall assess, then, at the end of the term is if this instrument of social integration improved the living conditions of the applicant. The models constructed in this context have the same binary response, but with a different meaning. Information such as the minimum income available, the number of dependent children and the reasons that led a person to apply for a microloan contribute to the search for an answer to the following questions: "Can microcredit successfully meet the unexpected financial need?" and "Can this tool restore the pre-crisis situation of a family?". The solutions to these questions can be found by estimating the probability of the success of this tool in the evaluation of the request. The expected value can then be compared with the results actually obtained at the end of the relationship between the institution and the applicant. At this point, it will be possible to establish the efficiency of the tool.

4.3 Microcredit in Sri Lanka, Peru and Benin: three comparison cases

In addition to the issues mentioned in the previous paragraphs, other issues relate to the socio-economic and cultural life of the destination country. If you look at the countries of the third world or developing countries, it is easy to see that they are mostly ex-colonial countries, where independence was gained by force and where, after the departure of the former colonialists, there have been clashes for the control of the country.

To achieve the democratic model there has taken years and, in some cases, repeated coups. Some of these countries have yet to take the first steps towards democracy, while others are halfway. Moreover, gender discrimination is still present. While in India, women have always had the chance to learn a trade and work, in Benin, for example, women are subject to discrimination with a capital D. In Peru, the situation is even more serious; in fact, women are heavily discriminated against and they have no right to education or health services. Health services are accessible, but not free, for women who are born in the big cities, but for all others, they are only a mirage. Many women in Peru still die during pregnancy or childbirth. According to government estimates of 2010, 185 women were killed for every 100,000 births owing to consequences related to childbirth or pregnancy. According to the United Nations Report 2010, maternal mortality could be more serious, up to 240 per 100,000.

In Benin, this violation of rights is now enshrined in all the papers that Western democracies even consider themselves to be discriminated against more than men, however fit the traditions of opportunism and the convenience of the moment. In this situation, it is likely that women are unable to see themselves as a force that when combined can sweep away the old sexist traditions. This section therefore analyzes three different cases located in three continents that have the highest rates of poverty: Asia, Africa and Latin America.

In the first, Sri Lanka, a country where small loans have long been a reality, microcredit was engaged in reconstruction after the disaster of the tsunami in 2004 and there women have access to high offices of state. The second is the case of Peru, where as mentioned, microcredit has long been established at the institutional level. In our case, however, you want to highlight the microcredit programs of the local Caritas, which are closer to the initial idea of Yunus. Peru is also a former colony upset by political turmoil since independence. Here, too, women are the main recipients of microcredit delivered by non-profit associations or NGOs. The third is the case of Benin. Here, attention is paid just to women, the main recipient of microcredit, but with cultural issues that do not allow making the leap to the next level.

4.3.1 The case of Sri Lanka

Sri Lanka, officially the Democratic Socialist Republic of Sri Lanka, formally known as Ceylon (official name until 1972), is an island located in Asia off the southeast coast of the Indian subcontinent. Owing to its particular shape and proximity to the Indian coast, it has been dubbed the tear of India. Its administrative capital is Sri Jayewardanapura Kotte, located 8 km east of the former capital, Colombo, which remains the largest and most economically important city in the country.

After the Portuguese (1597–1658) and Dutch (1658), the country passed in 1796 to the rule of the British, from which it separated permanently in 1948. Since independence, the conflict between the Tamil minority and Sinhalese majority has gradually worsened, leading to the civil war that bloodied Sri Lanka for the past thirty years. In the process of the escalation of the conflict, the number of political and military figures has increased and with it the weight of nationalism of a religious nature and new and extreme forms of violence such as suicide bombing and the use of children soldiers.

In 2002, with the signing of the ceasefire, the peace process between the government and Tamil guerrillas (represented in particular by the LTTE, the Liberation Tigers of Tamil Eelam, led by Anton Balasingham) was launched. This started a political dialogue between the parties and the reduction of the economic embargo that lasted seven years to areas of the north-east of the country. However, tensions between the majority Sinhalese and Tamil minority erupted into violence in the mid-eighties as a result of an attack on Sinhalese soldiers by the LTTE. This led to riots, with the deaths, in just three days, of 1000 Tamils in Colombo, while many others became refugees. Tens of thousands of people died in the ethnic conflict.

In December 2001, after twenty years of struggle, the Tamil Tigers and the government jointly signed a truce, with Norway as a mediator in the peace process. The Tamil Tigers have been declared a terrorist organization by the United States, the EU, Australia, India and Canada. President Chandrika Kumaratunga has admitted to the UN that there is deep-rooted discrimination in Sri Lankan society that leads to terrorism, but so far nothing has been put in place to ensure equality for the Tamil population (The Economist, 2007).

On 26th December 2004, the southern and eastern coasts of Sri Lanka were devastated by a violent tsunami. Estimates suggested around 40,000 deaths, although it was difficult to establish the exact number of victims. Following the difficult situation created by the tsunami, clashes between the Tamil Tigers and the military weakened the economy dramatically. This situation of extreme shock was skillfully used by a small circle of influential businessmen in the country to approve various laws of a liberal character, which have led to the substantial privatization of both companies and land.

The new zoning of coastal areas has prevented the reconstruction of houses and marinas previously destroyed by the tsunami in favor of the construction of new tourist facilities. The majority of the population that was sheltered in temporary camps inland could not return to their coastal areas of origin, losing not only their land but also their only source of income, which was fishing. These adverse events have rekindled the spark of ethnic clashes. In any case, the majority of Tamil coexists peacefully with the majority Sinhalese present within the country, except for the separatists in the north of the country where with Tamil Eelam they have formed a state of police forces, justice and taxation.

The military organization during the attack on Colombo in March 2007 could also count on an unknown number of light aircraft modified to carry bombs. These aircraft belonged to the "Air Tigers", the air component of the Tamils. The Tamil Tigers have already completed successfully daring naval raids with the use of small boats, explosives and suicide bombings, but these air operations showed a much higher level.

Since 2007, the president of the country has been Mahinda Rajapaksa, leader of the Freedom Party, with nationalist-socialist views contrary to concessions and to federalism in the country. The Tamil Tigers want autonomy in the northern region, where the city of Jaffna is considered to be a stronghold of the Tamils. If they got independence, they would declare a state of Tamil Eelam.

The President of the Republic, elected directly by the people for a term of six years, is both head of state and head of government in addition to being the commander in chief of the armed forces. The president is responsible for acting in front of the parliament, which can remove him from office by a vote of two-thirds of the members of the Supreme Court and the competition. The president appoints and heads a council of ministers. The vice president is the prime minister, who leads the majority party in parliament. The Parliament of Sri Lanka is unicameral, consisting of 225 members elected for a term of six years under a system of proportional representation by universal suffrage. The President may summon, suspend, or terminate a parliamentary hearing and dissolve parliament at any time if it's been in office for at least one year. The parliament has legislative power. Sri Lanka is a former member of the Commonwealth.

Before December 26th, 2004, Sri Lanka was presented as a state of "medium development" based on economic and social indicators that showed a growing country with good prospects for the future despite widespread poverty and numerous structural problems of a political, economic and social kind.

Sri Lanka is, for example, among the countries of Southeast Asia that have most promoted investment in so-called "social" issues, particularly those aiming at the enhancement of human resources and social capital as well as the promotion of gender equality and equal opportunities. These policies have allowed the achievement of positive results in several variables of human development, particularly health and education, where performances were more significant than those recorded in countries with higher incomes per capita (The Economist, 2007).

4.3.1.1 The tsunami of 2004

The history of Sri Lanka is characterized by serious tragedies that are the result of the colonial legacy of fragmentation, the radicalization of ethnic relations and militant interpretation of religious philosophy. The social and economic burden of the long conflict has certainly slowed the development of the country, keeping it below the average of the area and its potential. However, in recent years, the military truce and the start of dialogue have favored domestic and foreign economic growth, giving satisfactory results in terms of development.

The terrible tsunami that hit the coast of Sri Lanka in 2004 swept away the progress made, claiming victims and causing destruction and serious economic and social damage. When you consider that coastal areas are the most populated and economically most active in the country, you have an idea of the very serious consequences of the event.

The tsunami also introduced elements of instability into an already fragile political and social framework. Therefore, the structural problems of the local environment that existed prior to the emergency caused by the tsunami were compounded by the needs caused by the occurrence of the adverse event. Data on displaced persons and damage remain highly uncertain: the displaced vary, for example, depending on the source, from 570,000 to 830,000. The figures are obviously "flawed" by the difficulties of detection and, above all, the inability to distinguish displaced persons in camps, on makeshift beds or with relatives.

The districts characterized by major disasters were those of Batticaloa, Ampara, Galle, Matara and Trincomalee, followed by Jaffna and Kilinochchi, Gampaha, Kalutara and Colombo. Although there is no accurate data, drought has certainly worsened the living conditions of the poorest sections of the population and, with it, the most vulnerable segments such as children and women. Local and international organizations estimate about 1,100 orphans of both parents and between 3000 and 4000 who have lost one of their parents (Antonelli, 2005; Becchetti and Castriota, 2011; Becchetti, Castriota, and Conzo, 2012).

4.3.1.2 Microcredit in Sri Lanka

The first credit unions officially recognized in Sri Lanka date back to the early 1900s and thus they are the oldest form of cooperatives in the area. Often groups of this kind already existed, since the practice of mutual economic aid is historically widespread and deep-rooted in the country. For this reason, these organizations are characterized by a vitality and stability rarely found in other types of cooperatives.

Another peculiarity is the prevalence of women members rather than men because of the active role that women in Sri Lanka have always had in the home and in the family. Through the practice of credit, women are able to allocate the resources of the family for constructive purposes, often without their husbands if they are a negative influence.

Currently in Sri Lanka, microcredit is practiced within various sectors (e.g. rural banks of Multi Purpose Cooperative Societies, the Indiwara Banks belonging to the fishing cooperatives). However, two organizations are leaders in the field. These deal specifically with microcredit and play a particularly important role throughout the national territory. First, Sanasa (Thrift and Credit Societies) coordinates 8400 cooperatives spread throughout the country, with a total coverage of about 850,000 households. Until the 1980s, the structure was organized to accommodate basic companies such as coordinated local Credit Unions, which in turn were managed by the national organization of SANASA.

Since the 1990s, property has been renovated and organized units networked together, each with its own identity and function. The Sanasa Development Bank, a real bank independent of the Federation, is now an important financial organization. Its importance has grown steadily thanks to the efficiency of its collection of loans, which has led to an expansion of the operations into credit unions.

Figure 8 - Map of Sri Lanka

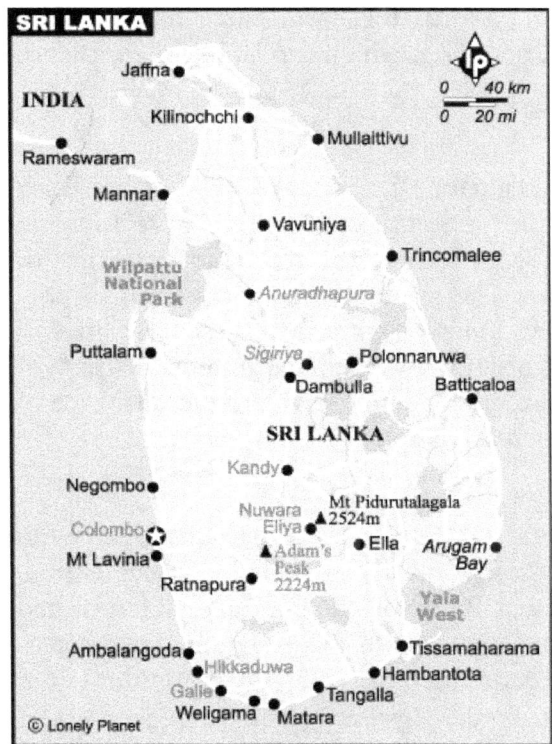

Source: Lonely Planet

This direct relationship, which bypasses the credit unions, has weakened them and they now feel threatened. At the national level, credit unions in some districts disappeared and a new national coalition of credit unions that do not want to lose their positions acquired in recent decades was born.

The Federation now supports direct contact between the Sanasa Development Bank and Sanasa base, recognizing the appropriateness and efficiency of the financial report with respect to Credit Unions. The staff of the latter, in fact, is not specifically trained to perform this task, since members are elected by the primary societies, which can lead to a conflict of interests.

In the aftermath of the tsunami, the Sanasa Development Bank started a rehabilitation program called the "Post-Tsunami Revival Program" in order to help the return to normality of the companies affected. The program was part of a loan pool funded by international donors, with access to several lines of subsidized loans. This program was applied in most districts of the country, with the exception of those where the influence of credit unions was particularly strong.

In the district of Kalutara, credit unions affiliated with SANASA relate financially mostly with the District Union. The Sanasa Development Bank, on the contrary, is not rooted in the territory and did not initiate the program. Here, post-tsunami aid was managed directly by the Federation through a rehabilitation program funded by the Asian Confederation of Cooperatives Union, for a total of 8,713,850 Rupees.

This program in 2005 reflected the following activities:

Additional contribution, varying from 1,500 to 3,000 rupees, to the General Managers of cooperatives for six months to prevent them from neglecting their duties.

Reconstruction of premises affected by the tsunami and supply of furniture through the construction sector of SANASA and SEDCO.

In 2006, the Federation expressed its intention to coordinate with the Sanasa Development Bank in order to introduce a line of soft loans for members with a minimum interest rate, partly funded by the remaining program budget of the Asian Confederation of Cooperatives Union. Given the enormous number of SANASA members affected by the tsunami in the district, this constituted the ideal continuation of the rehabilitation program of emergency first realized in this first phase project funded by LEGACOOP.

The Women's Bank was recorded in 1991 as a first level cooperative, in the district of Colombo. During the 1990s, the organization welcomed groups belonging to other districts, including Ampara, Polonnaruwa, Gampaha and Kalutara, until the successful decentralization and renewal of the Statute. In 1998, the organization was converted into the Women's National Bank. Since then, the movement has constantly expanded. It currently has more than 44 branches in eight districts, with 970 groups at 13,545 members, exclusively women in the weakest economic positions. By statute, the cell group of the Women's Bank is composed of five to 15 women members, who decide to form a consortium, setting aside at least 5 rupees per month. The group is headed by a president, secretary and treasurer elected democratically.

The capital flow is used to grant loans to other members through the circles of revolving funds. In practice, there is no capital left in the store, but the entire amount is circulated within the group. If at least 10 cell groups decide to federate with each other, to form a subsidiary (pradeshikaya) of the Women's Bank, with its own bank account, they can receive funding from the headquarters of the Women's Bank. The Steering Committee is composed of the treasurer of the respective organizations, which meet weekly.

The national body of the organization is the National Council, represented by the treasurer of all subsidiaries, with the task of formulating guidelines for the movement, providing financial education, providing basic equipment to affiliated and managing external financial sources. The National Executive Council has the task of putting into practice the decisions of the National Council and is composed of the representatives of the district treasurer. At the head of the National Executive Council is the General Manager, the only figure salaried full-time in the entire organization (Becchetti, Castriota, and Conzo, 2012).

4.3.2 Microcredit in Latin America: The case of Peru

Peru is also a former colony that since independence, like Sri Lanka and Benin, has experienced turbulent political moments. On July 28th 1821, General José de San Martín, in command of the expedition Liberation of Peru from Chile, declared the independence of Peru. However, the situation remained unstable and the actual liberation of the country was only completed in December 1824, when General Antonio José de Sucre defeated the Spanish troops at the Battle of Ayacucho. Nevertheless, it was only in 1879 that Spain recognized the independence of Peru. Therefore, Peru began to form under the protectorate of José de San Martín through the establishment of a Constituent Congress. The war against Spain ended, under the command of Simón Bolívar, with the campaign of Junín and Ayacucho in 1824, in which it finally defeated the royalist army of Peru

The independence of Peru is one of the many chapters of the wars of Hispano-American emancipation, which began in 1808 and ended in 1829, and which saw the Spanish monarchy clash with the nascent Latin American states who demanded independence. The early years of independence were, as mentioned, somewhat chaotic and characterized by petty wars for power.

In 1845, Ramón Castilla seized power, at which point he started talking about a democratic Constitution that was later enacted in 1860. In 1919, Augusto Leguía y Salcedo came to power and established a military dictatorship, the first of a long series, until, in 1939, the banker Manuel Prado Ugarteche became president. In 1948, a military coup brought to power Manuel Arturo Odría, who outlawed political parties.

The recent history (1980–2000) was also characterized by the clash between the Peruvian and two armed groups of the left: the Maoist Shining Path militants under the leadership of Abimael Guzmán and the Movimiento Revolucionario Túpac Amaru, commanded by Víctor Polay Campos.

Figure 9 - Peru

The Truth and Reconciliation Commission, created in 2000 to determine the effects of the war, concluded in 2003 that this internal conflict claimed the lives of 70,000 people, mainly in Andean areas and Quechua speakers. In 1990, Alberto Fujimori was elected, and on April 5, 1992, he dissolved Parliament and established martial law. In October 1993, he passed a new constitution, which enabled the possible re-election of the president for two consecutive terms, greatly expanding his powers. In 1995, Fujimori was re-elected president and, during this term, his country was engaged in armed clashes with Ecuador; only in 1998 did he sign a treaty that brought peace (Accorinti ì - ì Mirabile - Romano - Sgritta. 1998).

At the end of the nineties, the most important means of communication were controlled by the government to facilitate the re-election of Fujimori, who had already formed a vast network of corruption from presidential adviser, Vladimiro Montesinos, who was the head of the intelligence services. In 2000, there were new presidential elections and a new victory of Fujimori, who surrounded himself with vote-rigging and corruption scandals. In November 2000, Fujimori traveled to Brunei to attend the summit of the Asia-Pacific Economic Cooperation and did not return to Peru. Instead, he stopped in Japan and gave up the presidency by fax. In 2002, Alejandro Toledo Manrique was elected as President of the republic moderate. In 2006, new presidential elections were celebrated. On June 4, there was a round of balloting, which saw the dominance of the social democratic candidate Alan García - now in his second presidential term – and the nationalist candidate and anti-neoliberal Ollanta Humala. In 2010, the presidential election was attended by Humala and Keiko Fujimori, daughter of former President Alberto. The former won and today is the current president of Peru. In addition to a long history of political instability that easily creates pools of poverty, Peru has been devastated by numerous earthquakes.

4.3.2.1 Women and microcredit

Even in Peru, microcredit provided by associations or non-profit organizations is intended for women. Italian Caritas have since 1999 been working with the Caritas of Tacna y Moquegua in Peru to develop microcredit for microenterprises and small businesses; 80% of the beneficiaries are women.

The microcredit program began in August 1997 by the Caritas of Tacna, with funds from the Caritas Peru, awarded in the form of loan for $101,000 US. This activity was born from the withdrawal of the sources of cooperation given by USAID, which had direct assistance programs in health and food. The beneficiary population was initially localized in marginal urban areas in order to subsequently extend support in rural areas.

The main features of this microcredit are as follows:

-It is aimed especially at women

-Informal activities increase their working capital and improve economic revenue;

-The interest rate is lower than those offered by formal and informal credit to people with lower incomes.

Microcredit is for those who have:

-A minimum monthly income (less than 100 dollars) and a development perspective;

-Knowledge of an economic activity to develop, which can be of commercial type, manufacturing or services;

-Permanent residence (people have to live on a permanent basis in the home they report);

-The ability to form a solid group of 3–5 people who know each other without being relatives or neighbors;

-Morally reliable.

The programs undertaken by Caritas of Tacna included:

-The program for the reconstruction of living units: With funds from the Italian Caritas, this will benefit 69 families affected by the earthquake of 2001 for which 40% of the investment was signed in the form of credit, to be devolved in a time interval of 5 years at an interest rate of 22% per year in Nuevos Soles

-The program for the reconstruction of housing units along with the program for the promotion of the most vulnerable of society: With funding from Caritas Germany, this benefits 22 families affected by the earthquake of 2001, with preferential attention to people with activity limitation and the elderly, for which 20% of the investment was signed in the form of credit to be devolved in a time interval of 5 years at an interest rate of 22% per annum in Nuevos Soles

-The program of social and economic reconstruction: with funds from the Caritas, offers vocational training, aimed especially at women, through three training modules: technical production, business management and human development.

The project also includes the promotion of micro-enterprises, which develop customized technical assistance activities, organize trade fairs that sell products at the local level and strengthen *microimpresariali* organizations (Miglietta, 2004).

4.3.3 Microcredit in Africa: the case of Benin

The Republic of Benin is a country in Western Africa also known as Dahomey. It overlooks the Gulf of Benin, where the coastline is about 120 km, is bordered to the west by Togo, to the east by Nigeria and to the north by Burkina Faso and Niger. Do not be confused, however, with the kingdom of Benin, also known as the kingdom of Edo, which is now gone, and which originated in the area west of the delta of the Niger River. Of this kingdom, only the state of Edo remains today as part of the Federal Republic of Nigeria with Benin City as its capital. Benin is a presidential republic, the capital is Porto-

Novo, but the seat of government is Cotonou. Benin is a member of ECOWAS.

The name Benin relates to the Kingdom of Benin and Benin City, which took its name from the bay on which present-day Benin faces. The name Dahomey was changed in 1975 to the People's Republic of Benin, which was chosen for its neutrality, since the country is home to more than fifty different linguistic groups and nearly as many ethnicities. The name Dahomey was one of the ancient kingdom Fon, and it was considered to be inappropriate to define the whole nation. The African kingdom of Dahomey originated in Benin. In the seventeenth century, the kingdom, ruled by an Oba, spreading beyond its current boundaries, covering a large part of West Africa. The kingdom was prosperous and established relationships for the slave trade with Europeans, particularly the Portuguese and the Dutch who first arrived here in the late fifteenth century.

Figure 10 - The Republic of Benin

Source: www.elezioninews.it

In the eighteenth century, Dahomey started to fall apart, thus giving the opportunity to the French to take control of the area in 1892. In 1899, the territory became part of the colony of French West Africa, still under the name Dahomey. In 1958, it was granted autonomy as the Republic of Dahomey, and full independence followed in 1960.

As in ex-colonial countries with independence, there were turbulent times marked by coups and regime changes before Mathieu Kérékou took power. Considering the extreme poverty of the country, he established a Marxist regime. Thus, the People's Republic of Benin was born. At the end of the eighties, Kérékou abandoned Marxism and decided to restore democracy. He was defeated in the elections of 1991, but returned to power with the vote of 1996. Since 2006, the president has been Yayi Boni. The last presidential elections took place in 2011, which saw the re-election of Boni.

In Benin, there are about 40 different ethnic groups: the largest is the Fon, which comprise about 40%, followed by the Yoruba (12%), the Adja (11%) and the Somba Ani (5%). The first thing that strikes visitors about Benin is the impressive number of markets, vendors and stalls. As you walk the streets and markets that are everywhere, it is easy to see that the crowd is made up mostly of women with children in tow, often with one of them on her back and carrying heavy merchandise that towers on their head and moving, elegantly, in search of customers. However the woman in Benin have been subjected to a long period of discrimination, most tolerated or ignored by local laws since they are traditional customs to which no legislator seems to be serious about ending.

Combating these practices is equivalent to questioning centuries of male domination. Yet even here, in the land of the Amazons, the oldest and most feared women warriors, women would have the numbers and economic burden to compel the negotiation with husbands, employers and legislators. According to UNICEF data available for Benin, 37% of women between 20 and 24 years of age were married or in a union before 18. Of these, 45% come from rural areas and 25% from urban areas. This geographical distinction is part of the different levels of education between rural areas, particularly in the north of the country, and the areas of the south, slightly more developed both economically and socially.

We need to remember that in Benin, as in many other countries in the developing world, traditional weddings provide that the man offers a dowry and this is one of the main reasons why especially among poor families trying to marrying off their daughters as quickly as possible is quite common. In this regard, one of the "sixteen resolutions" that customers must comply with Grameen in Bangladesh, provides for the rejection of child marriage commitment not to accept or offer a dowry in exchange for the marriage, in order to avoid that it becomes a matter of pure economic calculation. Finally, with regard to women's attitudes towards domestic violence, 60% of women between 15 and 49 years state that such violence is justified. This means that almost one in two women in Benin justifies the violence of her husband.

Regarding data on the health of women in the same age range, the spread of prenatal care reaches 88% of the women, the skilled care during childbirth is present for 78% of mothers. Births take place in health centers in 78% of cases, but nevertheless the maternal mortality rate remains high and the latest estimates say that the annual number of deaths from pregnancy-related causes is 840 mothers for each 100,000 live births, while 1 in 20 women are likely to die in their reproductive years. Further, an extremely low percentage of women use contraceptives, only 17%.

Faced with these data, we can see that an awareness of their own strength and their own social and economic burden is lacking. However, this awareness can develop through an adequate education, which allows them to be considered as people and not as objects owned by others. Unfortunately, the first step of discrimination is in that very system of education, which should trigger a process of awareness of their own identity and autonomy of choice. Unfortunately, in Benin it is rooted in the traditional culture and the feeling of submission to the man; this is so ingrained in the female population that education alone is not enough.

In addition, tradition is not nearly as immutable as it might seem at first sight, but it changes according to the needs of men. For example, even Muslim wives that should be protected by some Islamic laws such as those governing polygamy are instead at the mercy of new practices for which the husband brings home other "wives" without any consent of the first wife, without being able to ensure the livelihood of all, and often ending up leaving them to themselves, with their children, in order to seek a new partner. Another common practice among men is to use traditional rites and unofficial ones in such a way as not to be forced to sign any kind of document that can provide his wife a possible foothold in the event of abandonment by the spouse.

This creates many problems, especially following the latter's death, because, in the absence of written records, all women who have been companions, more or less officially, make claims on the inheritance and so do their children. The shame of abandonment then always falls on the wife, because the common belief is that an abandoned woman is guilty for some reason. People might think she was probably not a good mother, a good housekeeper or a faithful wife. Left alone and, in most cases, with dependent children, these women no longer have any hope of finding a man to take charge of their livelihood or their children's and are forced to reinvent a life out of nothing.

The study by Marie-Odile Attanasso helps us highlight some interesting data related to gender differences. First, it is very difficult to assess the real level of poverty among women in a family context, since the statistics are normally made on the standards of living of householders, except that the women in question are not, in fact, heads of families.

Secondly, the incidence of poverty varies not only by gender, but also according to the geographical location. The general analysis of Attanasso proceeds on two parallel lines: on the one hand, she analyzed indices of poverty in the rural departments of Benin (11 out of 12 because the department of Littoral includes in practice only the urban area of Cotonou), according to gender. On the other hand, she takes into account the indexes of poverty and their gender differences, but this time within the major cities of Benin (Attanasso, 41).

The most devastating poverty is concentrated in the north of the country, despite the higher incidence in parts of the south. This is partly explained by the greater demographic weight of the south, which is home to nearly three-quarters of the population of Benin. As for the other factors that determine women's poverty in rural areas, while gender, age and profession do not seem to have a decisive influence on the probability of women becoming poor, in urban areas two factors instead become decisive, namely younger women and those who have the ability to carry out work are less likely to become poor (Attanasso, 67).

The majority of urban poverty is in fact borne by women engaged in the informal economy. This does not mean that in the formal sector there are no underpaid women, but these are 'pockets' of poverty in a system that provides a reasonable standard of living. Attanasso says that microcredit can be a solution if not limited to the granting of loans to fuel the already saturated field of informal trade, but instead oriented and focused on the social advancement of women's groups and the development of entrepreneurship.

Finally, the importance that the government has for microcredit should be recognized. Among the Ministries of Benin, one was created "ad hoc" for microcredit; it is also the ministry responsible for the development of small and medium-sized enterprises and the promotion youth and female employment. Microcredit is therefore present in Benin and headed mainly by PADME, a government project incepted in 1993 (Projet d'appui au Développement de Micro-Enterprises), following a World Bank program.

The project funded by the World Bank with the technical support of the American NGO Life was meant as a social safety net, by trying to ferry to the private sector the many civil servants that lost their jobs due to the structural redesign of the system (Gentilini, 1995: 389). This project ended in 1998 when PADME officially became independent and started operating within the microfinance world under the PARMEC law defined within the UEMOA (Union Economique et Monétaire Ouest Africaine) of which Benin is a member.

In 1998, the Ministry of the Interior recognized PADME as a non-profit organization and it was recognized as a public utility by the government in 1999 with a Presidential Decree. The Association received from the Ministry of Finance and Economy, in the same year, the mandate to operate in Benin.

The objectives and mission of PADME are:

"The vision du PADME est que l'offre par le secteur de la microfinance, de services financiers adapt's micro aux entreprises et aux personnes à revenus faibles jouera an important role dans le renforcement et du dynamisme the efficacit 'des micro-entreprises. Cela entrainera une des conditions amélioration socio-Economique des personnes à faibles revenus au Bénin. Aussi en résultera-t-il une réduction significant durable et de la pauvreté a renforcement et de la croissance économique.

The PADME if women pour mission de rendre the easy accès aux services financiers et rapide pour les micro entreprises et toutes les personnes à faible revenu, en:

offrant une ranges variée différenciée et de services financiers aux besoins ADAPTES spécifiques spécialement de chaque groupe et au développement de la micro entreprise;

garantissant a durable accès aux services financiers de proximité à un grand nombre de personnes à faible revenu en tout the consolidant Viabilité Financière de l'institution". (PADME - BENIN, 2013)

In other words, they are trying to create access to productive credit for all Beninese micro-entrepreneurs and low-income people, providing diverse and differentiated financial services adapted to the specific needs of each production sector. This is especially so for the development of micro-enterprises and for ensuring sustainable access to financial services for a large number of low-income people, thus consolidating the financial viability of the institution.

The main agencies of PADME are located in Cotonou (seat of the General Directorate), Porto Novo in the south and Abomey and Parakou for the center/north. PADME provides two types of financial and non-financial services. The first corresponds to the five types of credit disbursed to the association. The non-financial services aim to "raise awareness and training to ensure good management of micro-enterprises". These training sessions are designed to give the potential customer all the information on PADME and its products and the conditions to which the credit is granted. In particular, the client is made aware of the importance of proper accounting, the separation between the company and personal cash savings and compliance with the commitments of suppliers. They are also provided with some basic notions of marketing.

Figure 13 - Results

Eléments	2009 Détails	2010 Détails	2011 Détails	2012 Détails
Nombre de nouveaux crédits octroyés	6 229	4 943	3791	3067
Nombre de renouvellement de crédits	23 646	24 157	23617	21 383
Nombre total de crédits déboursés	29 875	29 100	27408	24 450
Montant des nouveaux crédits	2 512 145 000	1 989 275 000	1 606 095 000	1 200 295 000
Montant des renouvellements de crédits	21 603 093 500	24 288 713 000	25 347 982 500	23 287 791 250
Montant total des crédits	24 115	26 277	26 954	24 488

déboursés	238 500	988 000	077 500	086 250
Nombre de crédits soldés	26 329	28 223	27 870	26 661
Montant des crédits soldés	19 688 955 800	22 857 859 340	24 807 228 500	25 659 245 000
Nombre de crédits sains en cours	26 871	26 404	26 178	23 543
Nombre de crédits contaminés non contentieux en cours	967	1 254		0
Nombre de crédits contentieux en cours	723	953	1 369	1 271
Nombre total de crédits en cours	28 561	28 602	27 547	24 814
Pourcentage de clients actifs femmes	64.01 %	63.44 %	62.68 %	62.23 %
Nombre de clients sortis du portefeuille	8 785	14 635	8 847	9 171
Remboursement en capital reçu au total dans la période	20 968 748 441	24 384 078 690	25 431 179 656	25 678 933 798
Encours de crédits sains au dé de la période	14 425 602 899	16 658 528 559	17 932 401 299	19 067 818 802
Encours de crédits sains à la fin de la période	15 720 145 649	17 939 644 467	18 104 974 227	16 440 909 310

Encours de crédits contaminés non contentieux à la fin de la période	474 653 491	693 422 214		
Encours de crédits contentieux à la fin de la période	473 878 425	630 619 571	974 843 821	1 067 651 711
Encours total de crédits à la fin de la période	16 668 677 565	17 939 644 467	19 079 818 048	17 508 561 021

Training sessions are collective and last on average two weeks for new customers and one week for current customers. The financial guarantees required by PADME are of four types:

1. Guarantee Fund: "all clients must deposit at least 1% of the amount received as a loan in a PADME associated bank, in a guarantee fund. The total amount of the guarantee fund is divided among the different repayment programs for the customer. The Guarantee Fund is retrieved by the client at the end of his repayments. Should the customer have difficulty in repayment, this fund will be used to cover all or part of the amount not paid."

2. Deposit: "to enhance certain collateral (e.g. unfenced fields) may be asked customers to make a deposit in amount of 1% of credit obtained. The deposit can be considered a guarantee fund additional with the only difference that the customer must pay them in full before you get the credit."

3. Warranty for death: "To protect against the risk of insolvency linked to the death of the clients, Padme has put in

place a system of guarantee for death and the premium shall not exceed 1% of the credit. For certain types of credit may be asked customers to take out a life insurance policy from an insurance company."

4. Collateral (fields, vehicles, equipment, etc..): "They allow you to reduce the risk of insolvency of the customer, not because they ensure the systematic recovery of the amount is not refunded, but because they provide a means to improve the reimbursement when borrowers are in difficulties."

As in Bangladesh, in Benin women also have to fight poverty, which, however, is not eliminated with injections of dollars or euros, nor with structural adjustment programs that have exorbitant costs. What is needed are programs that take into account the far-reaching socio-economic structure of the country, with realistic goals and dynamic and flexible systems, especially as the first enemy to be destroyed is the rigidity of the deleterious aspects of the traditional culture.

4.4 Microcredit as a breaking point

If you want the idea of microcredit to be exported where poverty is a major problem, then the concept has to be adapted to every country in which it will be used. Thirty years experience of the Grameen Bank has produced significant results; if, as critics claim, it has not fundamentally changed the global economy, it has certainly marked a breaking point between conservativeness in some countries in the developing world and the progressivity of others. The acquisition of new concepts, however, meets the resistance of tradition and therefore is slowed down considerably.

This applies to all countries in the developing world that are adopting this system to free large pools of the population from poverty. This is especially true among the cases analyzed. The women in Benin are in fact running the economy, but the political power and decision-making in general remains firmly in the hands of men. A turnaround can take place only by providing women with the right tools to begin a serious struggle, conscious and tenacious, against the excess of African human rights. To make them the protagonists of their time and to develop the country, it is necessary for them to understand how many resources they have.

Microcredit designed and taught by the Grameen Bank primarily serves this, triggering a virtuous circle that by providing livelihoods to women indirectly benefits the younger generation that depend on those women and mothers. The experience of Muhammad Yunus has shown that women in poor countries are willing to sacrifice more than men, and in the presence of economic aid are willing to manage it wisely and invest in their well-being, but also in that of their children. They run enormous risks, precarious health conditions, human trafficking and a lack of certain rights.

However, microcredit in Benin seems to be in crisis, a victim of selfishness and corruption. The image of microcredit in Benin is compromised and it is necessary to rebuild the trust of the people that had placed in it hopes and dreams of a breakthrough. Benin may not yet be ready for a microcredit system on a large scale. More likely, the actors of local microcredit care more about starting a profitable business that enjoys the favor (and funding) of international organizations rather than worrying about the real objective, namely lasting and sustainable development in parallel with the macroeconomic development, which can only be, at least for now, the sole task of the government.

The hope is that small local associations such as Donga Women (association of the provision of microcredit) and many others will continue in their work without falling into the temptation for richness. The idea of using microcredit to make a profit is undermining this new form of credit devoted to eradicating poverty in the world.

4.5 The controversial issue of profit and cost

A controversial issue that divides the operators of microcredit concerns the profit that you should take away from this type of activity. Some argue that making a profit is an essential element for the sustainability of microcredit. Thanks to profits, in fact, microfinance institutions can quickly become self-sufficient, expand and implement the quality of its services, quickly reaching a large number of poor people and becoming more attractive for investment from rich countries.

Others, including Professor Yunus, argue that the logic of profit is against the very idea of microcredit. Microcredit was created to help poor people and not to take advantage (as has happened) of their difficulties in order to get easy money. According to Yunus: "Many argue that the profit-oriented microcredit programs actually operate in the interests of the poor as well as the economy in general. [...]. The business model on which these claims are based is the traditional one which interprets the financial economy, a model that, in my opinion, it works fine as long as the loans are granted to individuals who are part of the rich or middle class. But I have serious difficulty in accepting justifications for the request of high interest [...] when it comes to customers that are really poor. My idea is: Squeeze all the profit they can from customers which belong to the middle class. Take advantage while you can, of your strong position in the financial market! But do not act the same way with the poor. If you give them money, do not worry about profit, but act so that they have the maximum amount of aid in performing the step that can bring them out of poverty. When they will be out, but only then, you can treat them like all your other clients" (Yunus, 2010).

By contextualizing the words of Yunus, we note that they refer to a specific business idea: that of social business, or a new type of company that meets the criteria of social development rather than the principle of mere profit maximization. One of the criticisms most frequently given to microfinance institutions is applying too high interest rates. Since the seventies, when microcredit was born, the bankers who have adopted it have been accused by many of being the new moneylenders, who take advantage of the needs of the poorest. The real questions about the effectiveness of microcredit arose in 2007, when a Mexican microfinance institution, Compartamos, caused a scandal in the financial world for its exorbitant interest rates. Interest amounted to about 85% of the loan and the institution invoiced huge profits every year, with a return on equity of 55% (see also the scandal of PADMA in 2006).

The Mexican case sparked a series of reactions among professionals and economists. We wondered whether the conduct of Compartamos represented an exception or whether such behavior was frequent in the field. Interest rates vary greatly among various microfinance institutions and is difficult to determine the optimum amount, or how high this should be in order to be defined as "excessive". It is not impossible, however, to clarify the trends in the future in this regard.

The interest rate required by microfinance institutions, although it has declined in value over the years, is still higher than that required by traditional banks. The reason why this happens is that the latter has lower costs than standard microcredit institutions. Granting a large amount of small loans costs you more than a loan of the same amount overall, but granted to a single customer.

Further, running a microcredit organization is on average more expensive than managing a traditional credit activity: you need a larger number of staff to create a personal relationship and a climate of trust with the recipients of loans and more customer information. Further, some institutions (such as the Grameen Bank) send officials directly to the homes of potential customers. These costs will inevitably be reflected in the interest rates, which must be high enough to cover all the expenses and make the institute autonomous.

In general, four components are included in the calculation of interest rates: the cost of debt capital, provisions for loan losses, operating expenses and profit. The component that has the greatest impact on the cost of debt for the clients of microfinance institutions is operating costs, which constitutes an estimated 60% of total costs. The high incidence of these costs is due to management inefficiencies. However, it is not possible to generalize this statement, because administrative costs vary from location to location. The trends, however, indicate that in all countries except those in South Asia, operational efficiency is increasing, mainly due to economies learning from their mistakes and improving their administrative bodies over the years (World Bank, 2010).

As for the cost of debt capital and provisions for credit losses, these are less significant in defining the cost of debt. More precisely, it is difficult to act on them in order to reduce them. Regarding the first problem, microfinance institutions, unlike traditional banks, have less control over the cost of their financing (they are considered to be price takers). The global average rate of default by microfinance clients is 2.3%, with peaks in Africa, which, however, do not reach the 5% limit beyond which a microcredit institution is likely to become unsustainable. As for profit, a reduction in profits, considered to be ethically acceptable, would result in a decrease in interest rates.

Another critical element for microfinance institutions is the procurement of funds, which determines the effectiveness of the services that they can offer and their degree of independence from the government or banks. Microfinance institutions operate like traditional banks, but do not have the same degree of recognition at the institutional level. In the face of the same type of activity, which differs only for reference customers and the figures provided, microfinance institutions often have problems finding the resources they need, and often these financing difficulties do not allow them to design their ideal financial structure.

A large commercial bank that decides to initiate an internal microcredit project will not meet many problems even if it is reallocating parts of its structure to this new project. By contrast, an entity or an entrepreneur who wants to start a project like this will meet many difficulties that hinder the success of the initiative. The use of debt to start a business like this is a risky road and not always feasible. The lack of collateral and object of the activity of microcredit make these highly risky projects for the banking system, which focuses on investment with a safe return. The problem is that microcredit lacks adequate regulation, which allows you to create a dedicated figure in the nation's system. This lack makes it too "risky" to allow microcredit organizations that promote it to appeal directly to investors through the issue of bonds.

Donations are a very common system to access the funds necessary for the conduct of business, but they have one major drawback. Microfinance institution cannot regulate the flow of donations they receive, and to make matters worse, they tend to follow a pro-cyclical pattern, where a shortage of funds is recognized only when the situation has become too critical. International aid is notoriously used to finance initiatives for social development. Therefore, microcredit institutions should benefit from such aid. Of these, however, only a small proportion is allocated to this sector. Yunus suggested allocating a proportion of the funds raised at the international level specifically to organizations that channel donations towards initiating and managing loan programs in order to avoid wastage.

Chapter 5

Microcredit in the West: the alternative to the monolithic banking system

5.1 The Western financial system and the reasons for its stiffness

In European countries, the banking system tends mainly to use and sell "ancillary services". Rare are the cases where there is focus on dialogue with companies or individuals wishing to open a business just starting out with an idea. If, in the past, the bank manager or subsidiary had greater opportunity to get in touch with its customers and provide loans and credit lines at its discretion, now those powers are considerably reduced after previous recklessness in granting loans, at least in Italy. In other words, the European banking system has undergone a process of separation such that decisions are made in an environment far from the customer. Whoever decides whether to grant a loan does so without seeing the applicant in the flesh, which results in a total lack of judgment related to the person.

Attention to the person is reduced to this degree in order to minimize the risk of the non-repayment of the loan and, therefore, to reduce "bad payers". Therefore, banks and financial intermediaries around the world make use of advanced quantitative statistical techniques. Before granting credit, analysts apply methods or statistical models to assess carefully the creditworthiness of each customer. To do this, the funder must have all the necessary information to define the risk profile of the applicant. This information is provided by the consumer himself or acquired from the various credit reporting systems in every state. Without some of these data, it would be difficult to obtain a loan.

In order to better evaluate the reliability of the customer, in compliance with the regulations concerning the protection of privacy and consumer protection, the information that can be treated include:

-Data on the type of contract taken out with the bank (credit amount, duration);

-Information regarding the financial situation, the outstanding debt and the trend of the past payments of the customer;

-Information concerning exceptional events that might affect the financial position of the entity or enterprise.

Sensitive information such as the race, religion and political orientation of the applicant, and those of a judicial nature, cannot be treated in order to avoid discriminatory behavior on the part of lenders. The final judgment about creditworthiness must be objective. In addition, sensitive data, when placed among other information, will be treated on their own without affecting the final decision on granting the loan. In most cases, however, the use of personal information is strictly bound to the consent given by the applicant concerned.

The statistical models applied for the elaboration of the information specified above provide a quantitative measure of the risk of the transaction. In other words, the results obtained are translated into a score, which represents, in terms of probabilities or forecasts, the creditworthiness of the customer. The combination of these techniques is known as quantitative automated credit scoring. It is an automated system adopted by banks and financial intermediaries to assess the consumer's creditworthiness. This system thus allows banks to develop standardized information related to customers and to make objective judgments on creditworthiness. The score built on the potential customer is then compared with a given threshold value. Only if the score of the customer exceeds the defined threshold value is the loan granted (the customer is judged as solvent).

Many banks and financial institutions also develop other tools (e.g. scorecards) to support the management of the institution as part of the assessment stages of credit risk. Scorecards accelerate the process of the selection of good and/or bad customers to set policies for the disbursement of the loan and the determination of its amount, based on the risk associated with the applicant. The development of a scorecard requires good skills in knowing how to use statistical models. The various financial services includes advice, but banks are often limited to mergers and acquisitions for larger companies, while the offer seldom goes beyond the normal transactional services and short-term credit (Limentani, 2003, 23).

The question that arises in the literature is thus: If the main functions of the banking sector, namely lending to businesses and financial portfolio management, are capable of giving increasing returns to scale, what factors might prevent the evolution and formation of a single giant "superbank" (Bagella and Paganetto, 2002, 145) that can also intervene when there are no strong guarantees? The trend over time has been to ask for more and more guarantees, regularly certified by competent bodies. From this point of view, many firms have a solid foundation for the development of ideas, but no guarantees that would enable them to gain credit from the bank. At the same time, the European banking system has found itself at a loss where instead there were firms certified guarantees but not in practice. This paradox in many cases, as in Italy, whose economy is based on small and medium-sized enterprises, has paralyzed private initiatives and therefore the sound economic development of the country.

In particular, Italy is known for having a bad relationship between banks and their customers, both businesses and ordinary citizens. This has led to considerable economic disadvantages for the country, most significantly a drastic reduction in the propensity to save. This is especially so after cases such as Parmalat, a company that was almost brought to bankruptcy because of the mismanagement of the directors, supported by the banking system. Even though they knew about the bad management of the company, they kept selling securities to small savers.

The Parmalat case was the biggest scandal of bankruptcy fraud and market manipulation perpetrated by a private company in Europe. It was discovered only at the end of 2003, although subsequently it has been demonstrated that the company's financial difficulties were already detectable in the early nineties. The hole left by Collecchio's company, masked by false accounting, was of about fourteen billion euro at the time of the discovery. On charges of fraudulent bankruptcy, Calisto Tanzi, the owner of Parmalat, was indicted and later sentenced to eighteen years' imprisonment. The failure of Parmalat has cost zero equity shares to small shareholders, while savers who had invested in bonds received only partial compensation.

Thanks to the so-called decree "*salva-imprese*", Parmalat was saved from bankruptcy and its direction was entrusted to the extraordinary administration of Enrico Bondi, who has partially healed the accounts (while still having to completely respond to the claims the old investors).

These scandals did nothing but damage the image (already historically mined) of investment and banking system in the eyes of savers. This lack of trust between banks and customers is one reason why the relationships between banks and businesses were fragmented and receiving loans from multiple banks was very common. Asymmetric information was a very prominent problem that increased credit risk, forcing lenders into shared management and the wide use of securities. An exception was Germany, where they were rare reports of clientele that were realized over long horizons.

Around the mid-nineties, with the change in the relationship between banks and enterprises within a context of radical regulatory changes and profound changes in credit financial organizations, the fragmentation of banks reduced and intermediaries became more willing to create lasting relationships as businesses grew (TARANTOLA, 2007, 14).

Relations between banks and small businesses shifted towards a model of *relationship lending*. In relationship leading, granting credit involves a relationship with customers and takes direct and confidential information that goes beyond that in the public domain by using existing contacts that know the loanee. This requires from the bank an adequate organizational structure to ensure the presence of employees dedicated to the management of the relationship and a control system that can monitor the relationship. Such a structure requires a more precise segmentation of customers through product diversification (CORIGLIANO, 2007, 34).

The model of relationship banking incorporates all those activities in which the intermediary bank invests in the collection of private information that, in an exclusive manner, is appropriate to counterparties, pointing to the long-term profitability that results from stable relations with pools of credit customers. Through the model of relationship banking, the opacity of the relationship information between borrowers and lenders is, to some extent, overcome by the production of information by the bank.

So that banks can extract value from the model of relationship banking, two conditions must be met. First, the bank must have all the information necessary to evaluate quantitative and qualitative ex ante credit risk, thus minimizing the problems of adverse selection. This means that there must be the possibility for the bank and the willingness on the part cf the borrower to act on reducing the information asymmetry between banks and firms. Second, the bank must have in the financing of district prisons all the information necessary to identify moral hazard on the part of the debtor (SALSA, 2005, 2). Thanks to the adoption of more stable forms and collaborative context information, this has encouraged the growth of business and reduced the risks for banks. In other words, the information resulting from personal knowledge has helped identify the actual riskiness of entrepreneurs thanks to the perception of "environmental signals" and the knowledge of the 'corporate history' of the same (TARANTOLA 2007, 16). The configuration of the bank–firm relationship, despite the limitations identified, has offered financial support to enterprises, regardless of their size and location. Credit flows in large quantities, especially in the medium to long-term, satisfying the demands of the application.

Further, changes in the economic, regulatory and institutional framework have influenced the evolution of the bank–enterprise relation. The liberalization of capital movements and technological advances have increased the opportunity to offer products and acquire the best technology, raising the level of competition. This has led to numerous mergers that have resulted in new organizational and strategic choices for banks.

Alongside models of federal aggregation, in which the local roots of the banks involved have been maintained and strengthened for the benefit of the local clientele, another kind of model has begun to gain importance. This is an organizational model based on the segmentation of the units for business areas (corporate, retail, private), causing the fragmentation of the investor–entrepreneur relationship (TARANTOLA, 2007; 19; CORIGLIANO, 2007, 46).

This fragmentation has led to the banking system splitting in two, meaning it is not able to efficiently affect the asymmetry of information between lender and investor and unable to meet the financing needs of the company. The banking system, which has always favored debt financing over equity financing, enjoyed an advantageous position that has reduced the incentives for greater efficiency in investment financing and led to the removal of significant resources to the industrial sector by reducing the opportunities for development (Bagella and Paganetto, 2002, 147).

It is easy to understand that in this situation there is no room for microcredit. The stiffness in the request for guarantees has made the fabric of credit highly destructive to the economy, especially where there is solvency, but not the stereotypical guarantees required by banks for access to loans. In this scenario, it was easy to turn to illegal loans and the development of usury.

In the relationship between banks and businesses, there is an inability on the part of the credit system to truly understand what the small/medium entrepreneur needs. In this context, the model of the "Hausbank" (translated house bank) in Germany is very appealing (LIMENTANI, 2003, 25). The system of relations between banks and firms in Germany has traditionally been referred to as one of the main factors behind the success of their process of industrialization. (Onetti and PISONI, 2005, 1; Andreani, 2003, 321–353).

The term "financial capitalism", coined by Hilferding in 1910, is still used to describe succinctly the model in which banks play a central role in addressing and controlling the industrial system. The specificity of the German model derives from the combination of a multiplicity of factors, which can be summarized as follows:

-Universal Bank. German law, unlike what happens in other systems characterized by a model of pure bank, allows banks to hold equity interests, including relevant dimensions, in industrial enterprises. Participation in the capital gives banks an influence over company decisions;

-High degree of concentration in the banking sector. The German banking sector has a high degree of concentration around the four major commercial banks: they are the traditional Big Three (Deutsche Bank, Dresdner Bank and Commerzbank and since January 1999, Bayerische Hypo und Vereinsban), which arose at the beginning of the nineteenth century, in the period of early industrialization;

-Hausbank. The bank–firm relationship in Germany is conceived and designed as a long-term relationship. This does not mean that German companies have business relationships with a single bank, but that, among the various financial institutions, only one usually assumes a role of reference for the enterprise: in other words, a single bank provides, in the medium to long-term, most of the credit and manages the financial operations principal.

-Proxies. Associated with the direct ownership of shares in the capital of companies, German banks flanked by the votes of the shares held by proxy (so-called Depotstimmrechte) have the opportunity to exercise voting rights on behalf of shareholders. This significantly increases their ability to control the investee companies, with greater emphasis on those with dispersed ownership.

Unlike the systems of Anglo-Saxon origin, the role of financial markets in the contribution of capital, both debt and risk, to businesses remains limited in Germany (Onetti, PISONI, 2005, 3). In the early nineties, it seemed that the German model was the most appropriate to meet the challenges of economically developed societies and that over time all European and international economies would have to make the cultural leap. This would create banks with an increased awareness of what it means to do business, taking bank–enterprise relations to a new level of quality (LIMENTANI, 2003).

Today, the Hausbank model no longer exists; the banks that mostly practiced it suffered large losses on loans and were downgraded by the rating agencies. "It seems, in some ways, that the banking system - especially the German one - has taken a step forward and three back, and that access to credit by small businesses today is harder than ever" (LIMENTANI, 2003).

It has been said that the Hausbank model is based on trust between banks and customers and vice versa. This type of bank is characterized by a deep understanding of the client's knowledge of the activity. Hausbank must act as a partner to ensure the financial viability of future projects; it should support the customer if he ventures into foreign markets and propose its own products and services, but only if they are in support of its activities and in its interest.

The key element that characterizes the Hausbank model is the aspect of counseling. For the resolution of problems affecting the company's management and business plans for the future (LIMENTANI, 2003), the characteristics of trust and openness and the continuous exchange of information imply that the number of counterparties with which you can maintain a relationship of this kind must necessarily be restricted. This explains how in Germany the phenomenon of multi-banked companies is much less widespread than in Italy. Italian entrepreneurs historically tend to run to several banks depending on their needs and the types of services and credit offered in order to choose the institution that provides them with the most affordable price.

In the Hausbank model, the bank proposes and develops together with the customer the solution that is best suited to his needs. If the customer is convinced, he will buy the service, even if another banking institution offered it at a lower price. While paying more than the single transaction in the short-term, the entrepreneur has an economic return in the medium to long-term in the form of unequivocal support by the bank with which he has worked steadily (LIMENTANI, 2003).

It has been claimed that only large banks are in a position to support the German model because they can provide a remarkable range of financial products and, more importantly, can afford to invest in training employees to become real financial advisers for businesses. Small rural banks and cooperative banks, while being physically closer to the customer, do not have access to products or possess the skills necessary to play the role.

The Italian banking world seemed ready to import from Germany this Hausbank model, although there were concerns about the poor level of preparation of the employees called to act as "advisors" to small and medium-sized enterprises and that Italian legislation had never allowed ordinary banks to conduct certain types of transactions that German banks did, in particular the recruitment of industrial holdings (LIMENTANI, 2003). The expectation that the Hausbank model would spread across Europe has been disproved by the developments of the past decade.

Large German banks had a relatively easy life, because they could always count on a consistent basis of demand and time deposits with which to subsidize other products and services that were less profitable or still under development. There was, however, transparency issues on the cost structure and this led German banks to adopt any type of product on the market.

Large banks and German listed companies ignored shareholders' expectations in terms of information and attention to the performance of the action. The main interests of German shareholders were to know that the company held large hidden reserves and that more than the stock price, management gave priority to the soundness of the financial statements and the creation of "*Substanzwert*", or "substantial value" in the sense of the maximization of shareholder equity. If the prospects of a return in the medium to long-term were good, the client would bear costs in the short-term. This focus on the medium–long-term gave the greatest benefits (LIMENTANI, 2003).

With the opening of European financial markets and the arrival of the euro, German banks got into difficulties because they could no longer cope with the need to devote more resources to organizational, managerial and financial products to all new and all development projects that were in the pipeline. Universal banks have been found to have cut-throat competition in each division and in each area, because they constantly had to compete with the best specialists in the market, and not only at the national level but now also at the global level.

The effort soon became unbearable and banks had to radically rethink their strategies. Then, began an era of restructuring that led to a kind of "poly-specialist" bank, that is a bank with fewer lines of business but a much more specialized offering. Large banks started to abandon some areas. Among the key factors pushing German banks to reposition was the increasing pressure on capital ratios in view of the changes brought in by the new Basel 2 rules (LIMENTANI, 2003, 28 ff.).

5.2 The alternative to financial system: usury and its victims

Usury is the application of interest rates considered to be illegal because they make it difficult, if not impossible, for debtor repayment, forcing him to accept horrendous conditions put by the creditor as the sale price to inadequate company property. Threats to physical integrity perpetrated by the creditor of the debtor and his family are an integral part of the phenomenon of usury. The first historical references to usury hail from Yunus's country and date back to 2000 years before Christ. Among the Greeks, widespread usury was condemned by Plato and Aristotle. It is also present in Roman law, which on several occasions intervened to regulate the matter and avoid abuse.

Today, victims of usury are usually people and companies in financial difficulties, which cannot access bank credit because of the awareness of the likely insolvency of those seeking loans. These people and companies thus find credit through unofficial channels. The lender, at usurious rates counts of recoupment in the event of the non-payment of the debtor's assets, accepts the loan even in these conditions.

Frequently usurers (commonly called loan sharks) carry out other illegal activities, from which they derive the capital they provide, such as money laundering or acts of violence to break the will of their victims. Sometimes, the moneylender already has a considerable personal fortune and is able to provide guarantees to creditors of a certain amount. Sometimes loanees just sign a surety bond to allow the victim to get a loan. The lender refuses to grant a loan to those who do not provide sufficient guarantees and/or future ability to repay, and the surety can open doors to credit. In this way, the moneylender may charge interest, without anticipating any amount.

Otherwise, the usurer could borrow money from a lender, guaranteeing it with his heritage, and turning the sums to victims at usurious rates. However, frequently borrowing large sums may be reported, and the moneylender must document the use of credit facilities. The moneylender is not considered to be a job according to law; therefore, it is not defined as a profession. The annual turnover of usury in Italy is estimated to be 30 billion euro and it affects 150,000 businesses. It is also estimated that 36% of that turnover is controlled by organized crime.

Most countries provide a rate limit beyond which the loan is called one offered by a loan shark. At times, the rate limit is an absolute value, whereas other times it is periodically updated by governments and "hooked" to current interest rates and changes in inflation. Where a limiting value is provided, it is often called the principle of proportionality at the current rates and conditions of the case, which leaves wide discretion for judges to interpret. Some jurisdictions with a rate limit that has a more liberal orientation provide for the nullity "*ab initio*" of contracts considered to have been granted usurious interest rates. In this case, the victim of usury is not required to return the loaned capital.

There is a proposal by the EU Consumer Credit Directive that suggests completely liberalizing the credit market with no limit to the amount of loans or interest rates applicable. The Directive would allow lending money across the continent, with the financing company headquartered in the UK, where the laws are much less restrictive than in France or Germany.

This would become non-compliant with Community law and the national controls on interest rates practiced by countries such as Italy, France, Germany and the Netherlands.

A substance not governed by the Community case is the validity of contracts based on certain clauses. In this sense, the laws that provide for the nullity ab initio of loans with rates above a certain threshold would retain their effectiveness in the national territory. In Europe, the threshold of tolerance is 30%, 50% in Italy, and refers to another parameter, APR. APR is a measure that continuously varies.

It is therefore clear that in the phenomenon of usury, both directly and indirectly, the credit system plays an important role, due to the request for guarantees and by acting in some cases as usurers. We must not forget, moreover, that until a few years ago, Italian banks were applying interest on interest, making the small investor or entrepreneur virtually unable to return the capital initially obtained in the case of delay or default. This situation has become very dramatic with regard to mortgages.

Thousands of properties in Italy have been repossessed and sold in judicial auctions. The owner, in a desperate attempt to save his property, asks for a loan from a loan shark who promises to save the property, when in fact the victim is simply exchanging the debt he had with the bank with one with a criminal. Many say that at the root of usury is a broken banking system that is no more than a legalized loan shark.

Recently, some Italian banks have been forced to return money to customers for having exceeded the threshold of the interest rate permitted by law, playing with decimals and the operating expenses of the accounts. Every three months, in fact, the Bank of Italy defines a rate threshold beyond which banks cannot go when granting mortgages, loans or credit. If the limit is crossed, customers have the right to ask for their money back. Banks usually fix the interest rate a few points lower than the limit, but then add on top of that generic costs and expenses that, when summed, do raise the interest rate to around 50%. A famous case is that of a food business that received a reimbursement of 197,000 euro by the Monte dei Paschi di Siena (ex Antonveneta) for the violation of the law on usury (MANSERVISI, 2013).

5.3 The salvation of the poor in the dream of a Bangladeshi: microcredit lands in the West

From the model of Yunus, in the West has landed microcredit is two main forms: "social credit", often referred to as "credit", and "credit for companies", aimed at the creation or maintenance of micro- or small businesses. Today, microcredit institutions are many and operate both nationally and internationally. Their mission is to promote social cohesion by providing access to credit for individuals with no collateral requirements.

In recent decades, therefore, microfinance has been used increasingly in Europe. Despite its internal heterogeneity, owing to the different legal systems and institutions of the member states of the European Union and to the different nature of the main entities operating in the microcredit field, microfinance has led to the development of an increasingly dynamic microcredit model.

Activities in support of the most disadvantaged social bands began in the second half of the 1800s with the small village banks created by Raiffeisen in Germany, the British Lending Charities and rural banks and cooperative banks in Italy. Although microfinance and microcredit, as previously mentioned, have deeper roots than the idea of Yunus, they are fairly recent experiences on the European continent, where they have found fertile ground since the early 1980s.

The first types of microcredit began in Eastern Europe in the years of the crisis and the dissolution of the Soviet system, encouraging, particularly, the development of micro-enterprises. Only later did it reach the Western regions of the Old continent, pledging to ensure economic growth and social cohesion.

The recipients of this type of loan, which aims to promote social cohesion, are identified based on the level of poverty. The European Anti-Poverty Network (a network of NGOs and other groups, established in 1990, constantly engaged in the fight against poverty and social exclusion in the European Union) refers to two levels of poverty. Absolute poverty refers to the inability for a person to obtain a given basket of basic goods and services whose consumption is necessary to live a decent life, while relative poverty considers the poor who owns resources significantly lower than those held on average by other members of the society in which he lives.

Poverty is closely related to the concept of social exclusion. This can be a cause and, at the same time, a consequence of the other. Social exclusion is complex, multidimensional and multilevel. It is multidimensional because it can be generated by situations characterized by low income, unemployment, a lack of access to educational and difficulty in obtaining adequate health and social services. Further, it is multi-level because the causes of exclusion may result from measures taken at the individual or national level.

Although social exclusion in Europe is difficult to quantify, various indicators are used to get an overview of the extent of the problem. Some of these are the unemployment rate, the level of education of European citizens, the satisfaction level of care and medical checks and the rate of people who do not use the Internet. Social exclusion, in turn, is both a cause and a consequence of financial exclusion. A person is excluded from the financial system when he does not have any access (or has only partial access) to the services offered by financial institutions in his country of residence. Access to traditional banking and financial services is a necessary condition for each citizen to be economically and socially integrated into society. In Europe, financial exclusion can also depend on other characteristics, such as the subject's age, sex, level of education, employment status and household income. Further, it is more likely to affect single-parent families, households without a fixed salary, women, the disabled, young people aged 18 to 25 years in Western Europe and people aged over 65 years in Eastern Europe, the unemployed, people with low levels of education, immigrants and persons belonging to ethnic communities and those who live in rural areas.

Thus, the microfinance sector in the European Union, as well as outlining microcredit, aims to improve the socio-economic conditions of the most disadvantaged and stimulate a network of synergies between public and private institutions, non-profit entities and non-profit organizations.

Among the major contributions of the European Commission to the spread of microfinance is its support to the establishment of the European Microfinance Network (EMN). The EMN is an NGO, founded in April 2003, which has 93 partners including microfinance institutions, research centers and industry professionals from 21 European Union member states. Today, it is one of the main actors in the context of microfinance in Europe. The Association aims to (i) support the self-employed and small businesses, (ii) disseminate the services offered by microfinance institutions, (iii) develop and consolidate training activities and assistance aimed at both companies that operate in the sector and the recipients of micro-services and (iv) expand institutions and their programs.

To pursue these objectives, the EMN organizes in European Union member states, candidate countries, and at the Commission and the European Parliament, a number of activities (workshops, research, analyses, seminars, etc.), in order to foster cooperation and dissemination among microfinance institutions. The EMN also periodically publishes reports on the European landscape.

In Eastern Europe, the microfinance industry is much more mature than it is in Western Europe. About 50% of the institutions in Eastern Europe provided the first microcredit on this continent between 1980 and 1996, while only 15% of Western institutions, at the same time, had distributed and disseminated this new tool in the areas of membership. The microfinance market in Europe is dominated by NGOs and foundations, followed by other non-bank financial institutions, credit unions and traditional banks.

The Community initiatives do not stop here. The EMN, along with the Microfinance Centre, Community Development Finance Association and other entities active in the field of microfinance, has participated in the elaboration of the European Code of Good Conduct for Microcredit Provision. The code originated because of the different regulatory frameworks of various European countries, and it outlines a set of expectations and rules common to all operators in the sector. For this reason, rules concerning the management of microfinance, risk management, governance and relations with customers and investors have been approved and recognized by the European Union as essential to the effective operation of microcredit.

The purpose of the Code is not to replace the existing regulations, but to establish a simple set of uniform rules to be followed for the conduct of operations and for the regulation of the institutions themselves. Recipients are not only those entities that provide microloans. Indeed, the Code is aimed at customers in the industry, assuring fair and ethically correct treatment to investors and lenders, guaranteeing compliance with the rules on transparency.

As the field of microfinance varies in Europe, not only from the point of view of the actors involved but also from a legislative perspective, not all the terms indicated in the text can be practiced by each supplier. To overcome this shortcoming, the Code states the specific institutions not subject to the clause in question.

The European Code of Good Conduct for Microcredit Provision is divided into five sections. First, "Relations with customers and investors" shows all the rules and obligations that entities operating in the field of microcredit must comply with to establish relationships with customers and investors. It also lists all the rights of clients and investors. "Governance" contains the rules that the management and board of directors of the paying agency must comply with. "Risk Management" specifies all common procedures to identify and assess the risks to which institutions are exposed and for microcredit providers to manage credit and fraud.

"Common rules for reporting" consist of a set of rules for reporting and disclosing financial and social performance indicators, which, if properly followed, ensure the transparency of the activity and facilitate comparisons between the performances of different entities operating in microcredit. Finally, the category "Management information systems" sets the terms to be observed as to the completeness, security and expandability of the management information systems of companies.

The EMN is not the only protagonist in the process of the dissemination and promotion of microfinance in Europe. Another network of equal importance is the European Financial Inclusion Network (EFIN). The EFIN is a non-profit, internationally recognized association established in November 2009 and managed by Réseau Financement Alternatif (RFA), the Belgian NGO. It is the result of a coalition of 36 European actors operating in the context of microfinance and constantly engaged in the fight to stop financial exclusion in 18 European Union countries. In this network are not only banks, financial institutions, NGOs and public institutions but also universities and research institutes, experts and professionals in the financial sector and consumer associations.

The shared objective of these subjects is the development and promotion of ad hoc measures to promote financial inclusion for the most disadvantaged sections of the European population. The achievement of this end is made possible due to the different activities (debates, research, workshops) organized by the network and to the dissemination of the results and information collected from the various experiences studied.

Three reasons led to the creation of the EFIN: (i) broaden knowledge on the concept of financial inclusion, (ii) involve political institutions at national and regional levels to ensure the better local development of adequate means of financial inclusion and (iii) create a place for stakeholders to meet to solve the problem of financial exclusion, fostering mutual learning about policies.

The EFIN is crucial for the development of microfinance in Europe, especially designing new services and tools to combat financial exclusion. The parties involved can expand their expertise in the field and meet new actors on the European scene. Together with the EMN, it also participates in the dissemination of microfinance and supports the integration of the people included in the two networks.

5.3.1 Consumer credit and differences to microcredit

Very often, we use "consumer credit" to indicate microcredit disbursed to individuals who need small amounts to cover unexpected expenses or to get rid of high household indebtedness. This association stems from the need for a person to apply for a small loan to procure essential goods or durables to heal a past debt situation (rental housing, households, unpaid installments for the purchase of a car) or to pay for essential health services. Nevertheless, in the context of microfinance, it would be more appropriate to define "personal microcredit" as "social credit", given its mission to prevent over-indebtedness and financial exclusion and promote the social struggle of people excluded from traditional banking systems.

Other important differences between the term "credit" and "social credit" reside in the main characteristics of the two instruments. First, as mentioned earlier, it is difficult to find a specific law for microfinance and microcredit. As sectors in developing countries after the outbreak of the biggest banking crisis of all time, the European Union is trying to regulate these contexts. The intention is also to ensure the uniform operation and management of similar institutions engaged in the provision of microcredit and microfinance.

Consumer credit, however, is governed at the European level by Directive 2008/48/EC of the European Parliament and of the Council of 23rd April 2008 on credit agreements for consumers, which shows the importance of protecting consumers themselves. The Community text was approved after a debate that lasted more than five years, during which significant disparities between the laws of different member states in the field of consumer credit were highlighted. The intent is to assist the creation of a modern legal framework shared by every European Union country, which contains tools for the protection and assistance of the consumer and a number of obligations and commitments that lenders must adhere to in the course of the provision of credit. An important innovation was the introduction of a mandatory evaluation of the creditworthiness of the loanee based on the information available. The second difference between social credit and consumer credit is represented by the diversity of recipients. Social credit is aimed at all persons who, in the absence of the requirements and capabilities required for the normal channels of credit delivery, cannot access traditional consumer credit. The third element of distinction between the two types of credit is the amount of loans disbursed. Social credit or microcredit is a loan amounting to a maximum of 25,000 euro, whereas consumer credit has maximum values much higher (up to 75,000 euro). Finally, the different guarantees required to obtain a microloan play a very important role.

When a subject is open to any organization entitled to provide microcredit, he must not have any collateral. The relationship that develops between the client and the creditor is based on mutual trust. This is different to the case for a request for normal consumer credit. To obtain this type of loan, you need to have security personnel on which the creditor could seek in the event of the failure to repay the loan.

Despite the crisis that hit Europe in recent years, causing a sharp increase in the rate of poverty and in the non-bankability of the citizens of major European countries, consumer credit is widespread. Non-payers see a drastic decrease in their "scores". The score indicates, in this case negative, the reliability of the client and it is achieved through the application of advanced scoring systems for assessing credit.

5.4 Through ethical finance: the initiatives of the European Union

Before connecting ethical finance to microcredit, we must highlight that there is no single definition of ethical finance. In general, this term is identified through two distinct applications of financial instruments. First, microfinance (especially microcredit) is addressed, as mentioned, to the weaker segments of the population. Second, ethical investment is the management of financial flows collected with instruments such as mutual funds to support organizations working in the field, sustainable development, social services, culture and international cooperation.

When ethical finance specifically and rationally pursues sustainable development for future generations, it is also defined as sustainable finance. The so-called "Banks for the Poor" are institutions working in the field of microfinance with micro credit as their most popular service. To emphasize its effectiveness, the UN declared 2005 the International Year of Microcredit.

Microcredit considers two categories of potential users: the socially excluded, particularly the unemployed, and micro-enterprises. The first are those who want to get out of economic hardship or switch to self-employment through a start-up, if possible. Micro refers to all firms operating in the European territory with fewer than ten employees and an annual turnover not exceeding two million. The goal of these businesses is to get microfinance in order to initiate plans to rehabilitate the business, ensuring sustainable development.

In recent decades, micro-enterprises have been pervasive in Europe. They contribute to the growth in the number of jobs available today more than that provided by large companies. Altogether, 99% of the approximately two million start-ups born each year are represented by micro- or small businesses. This has led to an evolution of the economy in the European Union. It has gone from an economic model driven by large industries to one tied to small businesses, working mainly in the service sector. This turnaround has sparked greater demand for microcredit, which has also contributed to the establishment of micro-enterprises managed, in most cases, by formerly unemployed people.

The result achieved has further emphasized the role that economic and social integration can play in microcredit. One of its peculiarities, in fact, is to offer, in addition to the provision of financing, non-financial services, such as training, support, mentoring and monitoring to beneficiaries. Despite initial indifference to the discourses and theories of Professor Yunus, the modern era has required the active presence of microcredit in Europe, thus generating a widespread distribution of this tool.

The European Union does not grant microloans directly, but it manages programs or initiatives that are made available to banks and non-bank funds to raise the resources needed to carry out microfinance activities. After obtaining guarantees, loans and capital, the "middlemen" may grant small loans to disadvantaged people or to micro-enterprises who request it. The European Union is committed to promoting initiatives to encourage financial institutions to provide microfinance to micro-enterprises. Likewise, the goal was to involve the United States in the 2007–2013 programming period, in the process of implementation in EU, national and regional policies and structural reforms aimed at promoting greater economic growth and an increase of employment.

In this way, microfinance institutions have been able to receive funding from various European sources, such as the European Social Fund (ESF), the European Regional Development Fund (ERDF) and the European Investment Fund (EIF), as well as from programs and complementary initiatives that help offset the high cost of ownership, improve governance and manage risk. These programs and initiatives include CIP (Competitiveness and Innovation Framework Program), JEREMIE (Joint European Resources for Micro to Medium Enterprises), JASMINE (Joint Action to Support Microfinance Institutions in Europe) and PROGRESS Microfinance (European Instrument for Microfinance). PROGRESS Microfinance, owing to its complexity and importance in the field of microcredit, is covered in the next section.

CIP has a budget of one billion euros and aims to facilitate the establishment of small and medium-sized businesses as well as help existing ones expand their businesses. CIP is particularly conducive to the development of innovative or high-potential companies engaged in the fields of renewable energy. The financial instruments that characterize this program are implemented and managed by the EIF and vary according to the different needs and stages of development of the undertaking concerned. As regards the only tool of microcredit, the CIP program offers support to European microfinance institutions to encourage actors, public and private, by providing small loans to micro-enterprises.

JEREMIE (Joint European Resources for Micro to Medium Enterprises) is an initiative that allows EU member states to access EU structural funds to promote and improve access to credit for small and medium-sized enterprises. Thanks to the collaboration between the European Commission and the EIF, microfinance institutions and the national and regional authorities of each member state may resort to the structural funds allocated to them, particularly ERDF finances for the creation of new small or medium-sized enterprises, the expansion of existing ones, research and development, innovation, entrepreneurship and productive investment in order to maintain employment. The contributions of the tools made available by the European Union are therefore designed to guarantee the funds used by microfinance institutions to invest in businesses. JEREMIE also intervenes in the activities of technical assistance and advisory services promoted in favor of micro-, small and medium-sized enterprises.

JASMINE is a pilot initiative launched in 2009 and developed by the European Commission in collaboration with the European Investment Bank (EIB) and EIF. JASMINE can be defined as the operating result of the communication of the European Commission on 13 November 2007, which proposed a "European initiative for the development of microcredit in support of growth and employment". By leveraging the existing cooperation between banks, often encouraged by public support mechanisms, and microfinance institutions, this initiative is divided into four actions:

"Improve the legal and institutional environment in member states": the premise is to increase the availability of financial resources in order to allow non-bank institutions and banks, which operate in the context of microfinance, to develop its microcredit projects without excessive costs. This European initiative also includes a reduction in operating costs through the application of more favorable tax regimes to aid the development of emerging companies, and a modification of the maximum interest rates on loans. Raising enough the interest rate will allow banks to cover the costs related to the management of any practice of microcredit. It also allows access to all microfinance institutions Europe-wide data, which contain information on loans repaid, or not, by individuals or by micro-enterprises. With this first action, therefore, the European Commission can categorize microcredit in the banking sector and new accounting standards, thus improving its sustainability and long-term importance.

"Change the climate to make it more favorable for entrepreneurship": when someone receives microcredit, he not only receives financial aid. This, if taken alone, cannot solve the problems. Through volunteering and the resources made available from the ERDF, ESF and European Agricultural Fund for Rural Development, the amount paid is accompanied by training, mentoring and technical assistance for new entrepreneurs. In this way, each person can improve the chances of the success of their micro-business.

"Promote the dissemination of best practices": through cooperation between banks and non-bank microfinance institutions, different experiences, skills and best practices are shared. In this way, banks can learn a lot from non-bank organizations, and vice versa.

"Provide additional financial capital for microfinance institutions": to enhance the supply of this instrument and to increase, therefore, the financial resources available, the European Commission proposes the establishment of a new structure-specific microcredit. This facility would target new microfinance institutions, thereby guaranteeing technical assistance for banks or microfinance institutions in general, the publication of manuals, guide and software and the organization of conferences and seminars and access to financing.

In continuity with all the elements of this initiative, the JASMINE program supports non-bank microfinance institutions, helping them become more sustainable and improving their internal processes. Technical assistance is therefore what is made available to institutions that decide to participate. In September 2009, there was the first opportunity for European microcredit providers to express their interest in receiving technical assistance. Applicants had to meet certain requirements:

-operate in an EU member state;

-operate for at least two years in the field of microfinance;

-have more than 150 active customers during the last year;

-be engaged in social action;

-demonstrate their internal strategy.

Following the selection of applicants, with the collaboration of one of the two rating agencies involved in the initiative, a number of estimates were made and judgments on the activities performed by the microfinance institution examined. At the end of these operations, areas and aspects to be improved were highlighted and helped to be solved. Once the process of assessing the performance of the microfinance institution had ended, each subject received a "label" as a testament to the quality of its processes. This label ensures good publicity among all those interested in the micro-tools of microfinance. Technical assistance is, of course, free for all institutions accepted to participate in JASMINE. Since 2010, 49 institutions operating in the context of microfinance and microcredit have received support from the European Commission through this program.

The definition of these three European initiatives, together with PROGRESS Microfinance, is very important for the creation and development of a more suitable environment for microcredit in Europe. These programs have also prompted many institutions to improve their businesses, mainly due to the ability to access the ESF and the greater availability of economic resources to finance business projects.

Among the most severe consequences of the current financial crisis are the almost complete lack of jobs and the high rates of social exclusion and financial barriers to access bank credit for micro- and small businesses and the unemployed. An important intervention of the European Union in employment and social policies was the definition of –PROGRESS. In line with the objectives of the Lisbon Strategy, PROGRESS supports the development and coordination of EU policies in five major sectors of activity: employment, social protection and inclusion, working conditions, anti-discrimination and diversity, and equality between men and women. It further supports the following types of actions for each sector of activity:

-"Activity analysis" consists of the collection, processing and subsequent spread of the data and in conducting studies, carrying out statistical analysis and calculating indicators, whose results should be disseminated in the form of reports, guides or other educational material via the Internet or other media support;

-"Mutual learning, awareness and dissemination" to facilitate the exchange of views and mutual learning and to organize conferences, seminars and workshops at the national or European level, contributing to the creation of partnerships and sharing valuable experiences;

-"Support for main actors": these are contributions to the operating costs of the main European networks, the creation of working groups to facilitate cooperation between institutions in different member states, networking among specialized bodies and observers at the European level.

PROGRESS aims to improve the understanding and knowledge of the social context of each member country, to offer analysis, tools, indicators and statistical methods, to support the implementation of the policy objectives and legislation in force in the country, to promote mutual learning through the creation of networks, to make known to each institution the policies of the European citizen and to help the main networks of the European Union in strengthening their capacity to support EU policies. Access to the program is intended for all organizations. The proposed budget is approximately 683 million euros for the 2007–2013 programming period, and it is almost equally distributed between the five sectors of activity.

PROGRESS Microfinance, operating from April 2010, has been developed as part of the wider program and is funded by the European Commission and the EIB, and managed by the EIF. It is the first program ever in the Euro area dedicated to microcredit for micro- and small businesses, thereby increasing rates of employment and social integration. Its mission is to make available to microfinance institutions, banks or non-bank, guarantee instruments and funding mechanisms. Guarantee instruments are issued by the EIF in favor of microcredit providers or guarantee institutions which, in turn, issue guarantees to cover risks of microfinance institutions. These instruments are intended to cover the risk for any losses incurred by microcredit providers.

In this way, the "microfinancer" is inclined to grant small loans to those applicants also more exposed to default risk, such as young first-time entrepreneurs or immigrants. In other cases, the guarantee is used to reduce interest rates on loans or to make less stringent requirements for participation. It is, therefore, a tool to improve the "contract".

Regarding financial instruments, the European Commission and EIB provide four types of loans and equity capital to microfinance institutions:

-Senior loans, simple to use tools that provide cash for intermediaries to increase their volume of loans;

-Subordinated loans, more sophisticated loans that allow a reduction of the limits imposed by the capital requirements that intermediaries must possess;

-Loans with risk-sharing, usually required by banks;

-Equity participation in the form of direct investment in a microfinance institution or indirect investment in a fund.

The guarantees and financial instruments made available by PROGRESS Microfinance are complementary. This feature increases the effectiveness of both these European initiatives if the activity is carried out by microcredit providers that use such tools. Progress Microfinance, therefore, does not directly grant microloans to small businesses, but rather finances microfinance providers with the resources made available by the main European institutions (European Commission, EIB and EIF), allowing it to increase the volume of loans available.

For the period from 1 January 2010 to 31 December 2013, the European Commission allocated 103 million euros, of which 60 million euros was for the creation of PROGRESS Microfinance. The EIB added an additional 100 million euros, thus ensuring a total amount of 203 million euros split between the two instruments: 25 million and 178 million euros for guarantees for the financial instruments. It is estimated that 203 million euros produces a leverage effect of 500 million euros in microfinance, or about 46,000 microloans.

Microcredit providers who want to become intermediaries for PROGRESS Microfinance must demonstrate their interest in security instruments or submit directly to the EIF demand for financial instruments. On the basis of the data published in the 2011 "Report from the Commission to the European Parliament, the EIF had signed 18 contracts with providers of microcredit members from 12 countries, eight non-bank institutions, seven banks and one public institution. These providers, until March 2012, had granted 2,933 microloans, of which 1,834 were in the form of guarantees and 1,099 financial instruments.

PROGRESS Microfinance is complementary to other European initiatives undertaken for the development of microfinance in Europe and the ESF. Some beneficiaries of JASMINE have turned to PROGRESS Microfinance, while various intermediaries who have obtained funding under

PROGRESS Microfinance have also applied to benefit from the technical assistance guaranteed by the JASMINE program. Many organizations in different states, however, ask for help from the ESF, which funds the development and growth of enterprises. For this reason, microcredit providers supported by PROGRESS Microfinance are often driven to collaborate with these organizations.

With about 200 million euros allocated for the period 2010–2013, they are still far from reaching the solution to the social and financial problems in European Union member states. Nevertheless, the financial intermediaries who express their interest in receiving assistance from the instrument will have guarantees and financial resources made available by the Commission, the EIB and the EIF.

As already mentioned, in every business sector in which it operates, the PROGRESS framework program funds a range of actions aimed at analyzing data and publishing reports related to its activities and objectives. All information collected and the possible strengths and weaknesses of each sector are known to those interested in these contexts through the organization of seminars, workshops and conferences, both at the national and at the Community level.

In this regard, in line with the need to combat social exclusion and to increase employment, a project co-financed by the PROGRESS program and the recently launched EFIN is CAPIC (Cooperation for Inclusive Affordable Personal Credit). This project explores and promotes four initiatives undertaken in the context of European social microcredit, which favor the integration of the most vulnerable members of a population. Its main purpose is to disseminate new models of cooperation that involves myriads of different promoters, including a public agency, a non-profit or a private company and a financial institution. CAPIC, therefore, aims to disclose in the European territory by using newsletters, training seminars and workshops, the good results achieved in the context of the social microcredit initiatives analyzed.

The project has a duration of eighteen months. It was launched on September 1st, 2011 and ends on March 1st, 2013. Partnerships analyzed during this period have settled in the geographical areas of France, England, Belgium and Italy, and have a bearing on both their own country and the European level. These can be considered to be good examples of European cooperation between parties who, motivated by the desire to learn best practices from other partners, reach a large set of potential beneficiaries.

The coordinator of CAPIC is RFA. In addition to the analysis, research and dissemination of the results obtained on the Belgian partnership in which RFA is actively involved, this NGO is in charge of the management and administration of the Community project as a whole. RFA has a direct and continuous relationship with the European Commission and manages the work, financial matters and liaison with the project partners of CAPIC. It also ensures the organization of meetings and creation of tools for the dissemination of information to foster mutual learning and knowledge on European activities engaged in the provision of social microcredit.

To ensure the effectiveness of CAPIC, in addition to the Belgian NGO, subjects must have long experience of the issues of financial exclusion and the provision of microloans.

The protagonists are, therefore, researchers, consultants, networks created for the dissemination of information, experts in the provision of microcredit and teams specialized in training activities and training the bodies involved.

Participation by all these actors in CAPIC ensures the achievement of significant results in every dimension of action, starting from the research of case studies, communication, training sessions and training of stakeholders to the disclosure of the success of the initiative. The specific objectives of the project are as follows:

-To promote the fight against social exclusion and ensure better working conditions in order to increase employment;

-To promote new models of cooperation involving government agencies, non-profit organizations and financial institutions. Each entity, in line with its objectives, will be able to reap benefits from participating in the partnerships;

-To encourage mutual learning and expand the provision of microcredit to beneficiaries. -To provide access to goods and essential services and ensure well-being and self-esteem to the most vulnerable in the population;

-To analyze the steps involved in CAPIC and ensure the dissemination and development of best practices;

-To measure the results of the effects of each partnership on their beneficiaries.

5.5 The characteristics of microcredit in Europe

The phenomenon of microcredit is acquiring characteristics in developing countries as well as Eastern and Western Europe. For poor countries, this tool has become in practice a form of access to credit involving large sections of the population. In the case of Bolivia, 80% of the population is served by the microfinance sector and not by traditional credit. Likewise, in Bangladesh, the Grameen Bank has become the fifth largest credit institution in the country. In Eastern Europe, microcredit is, broadly speaking, the only means of financing for small and medium-sized enterprises.

In Europe, the microcredit sector is young and rather heterogeneous, but growing because the development of the traditional banking system has given rise to a series of ad hoc tools that meet the needs of micro-enterprises, with the support of the state. However, this sector has erected barriers ever higher against persons devoid of all forms of guarantee that today allow access to credit. The organizations involved in the projects are diverse and include banks, NGOs, associations and government agencies with a strong predominance of non-profit organizations.

For several years, the European Union has supported and promoted the microcredit initiatives of member states, with the aim of encouraging both the launch of new micro-enterprises as part of the strategy to combat unemployment and the growth and development of existing ones. Small businesses often face problems related to investments both in fixed capital and in human capital: in this sense, the tight supply of microfinance instruments is one of the major obstacles to be overcome, particularly when the contractor is an unemployed person, a woman or an immigrant. This is why supporting microcredit projects makes it possible to sustain economic growth and social inclusion at the same time.

The role of microcredit is to be an instrument of social inclusion. In this sense, the activation of a series of relationships, namely "networks" in the territory that foster ties not only between the paying institution (or promoter) and the recipient but also with the community, is crucial. From the perspective of local development, microcredit should overcome the rather restrictive definition that reduces it to a loan for small entities.

At the strategic level, the most important issues for the future of the industry are related to the financing and sustainability of microcredit programs. In particular, the concept of sustainability expresses the ability of a microfinance institution to survive over time without being dependent on external aid and donations in order to ensure the continuity of the project. Concretely, a microfinance institution is sustainable if it is able to cover its operating costs.

Most institutions in Western Europe are highly dependent on both public and private resources to cover their operating costs: on the contrary, in countries in the developing world and in Eastern Europe, the size of the market available and the application of high interest rates compared with Western standards are the keystones to achieve sustainability. In Italy, in particular, the argument cannot be separated from the current legislation concerning the regulation of credit and usury: to date, a person who is not a bank cannot lend directly or collect savings. High operating costs represent a very strong cap on development in the sector and thus the ability to raise capital to provide loans is a challenge for the future (NARDONE and VILLA, 2008).

Chapter 6
Microcredit; microfinance and ethical finance in Italy
6.1 The banking system in Italy

The Italian banking system, since its birth in 1961, has been marked by repeated financial crises, and a close relationship with industry, which has led to the "mixed bank", first abolished and later restored (BALDAN, 2006). The birth of national banking systems can be made to coincide with the advent of the Industrial Revolution, although there are examples of activities related to currency and payment systems in earlier eras.

In particular, in the previous century, the Industrial Revolution in Europe saw many changes in the field of banking business through the development of the private bank, such as unlimited liability, limited partnerships and sole proprietorships. In the first half of the nineteenth century, new banking institutions that dealt with mortgage credit and the collection and use of savings were built. The explosion of these banks also put them in a position to financially support governments by granting substantial loans. In this way, states could finance revolutions and wars almost everywhere (BALDAN, 2006, 26).

In the first 20 years after the unification of the industry, it experienced a period of very slow growth. Only later, in the period 1881–1888, did growth intensify and then accelerate from 1896 until the First World War (BIANCO, 2002 14). Nevertheless, the Italian industry was closely linked to the agricultural structure of the country, especially the strong ties that much of the industrial labor force maintained with their peasant families. In addition, most of the industry was made up of small craft enterprises that worked at home. Only in more modern sectors was there economies of scale (BIANCO, 2002; 15).

In particular, the early stages of Italian economic development was marked by conservative economic interests, for which the system of tariffs distorted the balance between competition and monopoly in favor of more mature industries (wheat and steel) to the detriment of mechanical sectors. Italy experienced particularly strong industrial development in the late nineteenth century and the First World War. As for Germany, France, Belgium and the Netherlands, the pace of the industrialization process in Italy proved more rapid than that in Great Britain. This difference in the speed of development also involved both productive and financial training systems (BALDAN, 2006).

In Britain, the gradual nature of economic development secured the independence of industrial enterprises from the banking system. Central European countries did not achieve the same rate of economic growth and industrial yields were insufficient to finance this process compared with the gradual internal accumulation of capital in companies that characterized the financial structure of British industrial companies (BALDAN, 2006). These circumstances, such as the scarcity of money in circulation, gave rise to a different development of banking activity in much of the European continent: banking characterized by close ties between banks and industry, having first assumed the role of a "specific instrument of industrialization in a backward country".

As noted above, a banking system based on close ties with industry is easy terrain when there is a lack of circulation of money and liquidity, as was the case for Italy in the years preceding and immediately following unification. Italy in the late nineteenth century was the classic example of a latecomer country, with relatively late industrialization compared to other countries such as England. Before unification, manufacturing activity was poor, unlike the craft that was widespread. At the time of unification, Italy was a peripheral country in Europe: its total income was one-third of the French and one-quarter of the English and infrastructure projects were undeveloped, while the gap in the facilities of the manufacturing sector was even higher, resulting in high levels of productivity differences (BIANCO, 2002, 10).

The eighties were characterized by a profound change in the political climate. In different times and different ways from country to country, credit policy moved towards choices that favor the expansion of the market and a more reduced state presence. An ever-growing political faction was hostile to the presence of the public sector as a direct operator in the economy and, in parallel, the tendency to prefer control systems based on independent authorities that were deemed to be 'experts' in the sector. The main tool to reduce the state's role as an economic operator was in fact privatization.

After the interventions of the Banca d'Italia in the eighties, the real leap was adopting a new structure that all other banks were invited to follow: corporation (JORDAN, 2007). This invitation was taken up with the approval in 1990 of a law known as the Amato Law. This law introduced a new framework for groups of credit and public institutions. Once this step had been taken, they also pushed for public companies to adopt a private company structure. To do this, banks were encouraged by a series of tax breaks to make the transition to joint-stock companies, which opened the possibility for banks to raise capital to risk and encouraged recapitalization. (MASCIANDARO and RIOLO, 1997). The most important part of this law concerned institutions in the medium and long-term. In short, all the activities of special credit previously carried out by various institutes were merged into one group. In essence, while waiting for the universal banking model to be accepted, it allowed banking groups to complete the range of activities carried out within the group.

The change was radical: lending became an activity whose only feature was the recruitment of a prolonged financial commitment in time. The Amato Law allowed them to operate with medium and long-term credit and with no restrictions (GIORDANO, 2007). The possibilities offered by the Amato Law were widely implemented. About 35 institutions were operating by the mid-2000s, of which 18 were already part of banking groups owned by commercial banks.

With the Amato Law came into play foundations. This recognized the special role of banks compared with other companies in the public sphere, particularly with respect to the industrial enterprises of state holdings. The Bank of Italy notes, for example, the singular position of the Treasury that, in the case of the transformation of public banks into joint stock companies, would be found to be at the same time owner, supervisory authorities and, in many cases, the main debtor.

Public banks, therefore, required a true separation between management and control, which placed management outside of external pressure and made it subject only to the maximization of profits, under the regulatory burden imposed by the Bank of Italy. The choice that followed saw bank holdings entrusted to agencies that, although not entirely proper, became universally known as foundations. These, in turn, assumed the status of "public body holdings", which were a spin off from the banking business granted to a corporation of which the foundations in the first instance owned the entire share capital.

With the enabling law that accompanied the Amato Law began the tortuous passage from a formal privatization to a concrete one,the secondary aims for these entities - the public charity - became the primary. It severed, therefore, the organizational ties between the foundation and the banking group to the point that the foundations were no longer subject to the regulations concerning credit discipline with regard to areas such as banking supervision and crisis management.

The bodies had to redefine their goals, directing them towards public interest activities or social utility. This opened a controversial chapter that concerned the substantial privatization of banks, an area that caused considerable political resistance and significant delays compared with the original intentions. Yet, the separation between banks and industry had as its base a concept fundamental to the economic stability of a country: the logic of the entrepreneur may not coincide with that of the bank and the lender, which benefitted the profitability and growth of the industries themselves (JORDAN, 2007; BALDAN, 2006).

6.2 Microcredit in Italy

In Italy , microcredit is in constant evolution, taking, day after day, new characteristics and new responsibilities towards society both nationally and internationally .

Italy has been one of the countries that , since 2005 , the International Year of Microcredit , has responded more promptly and effectively, than most countries, to the appeals and the instructions of the United Nations .

With the creation of the Committee for Microcredit in 2005 , the establishment of a national coalition representing a plurality of members of the public sector , the third sector and the private sector, and its subsequent transformation into a permanent institution under public law, the country became one of the pioneers of modern microfinance .

This sensitivity is not surprising, since the phenomenon is part of the tradition and economic policy of the country, since the fifteenth century, where , although not yet a state in all respects (as it is known is the unification of Italy in 1861), in the Italian Peninsula , appeared the first pawnbroking , which, as mentioned earlier , were nothing more than financial services reserved for the poorer sections of society (BOCCHELLA , 2007).

Especially comparing our country with the U.S. highlights the different application of welfare : it is undeniable that in Italy even if a person is poor, healthcare will almost allways be available to them.

Even the deeply rooted Catholic institution promotes culturally and offers help to people in need through the capillary presence in society. There are numerous NGOs and associations in the country to promote volunteerism and solidarity.

Therefore we can say that Italy , at least theoretically , is more resistant to cases in which poverty could lead to misery.

Microcredit institutions also aim to help people, but with a different method: it doesn't provide relief only when the person is in need, instead, it aims to eradicate all the factors that have caused this need so that the person will never face the same problem again.

Yet according to statistics from RITMI "Rete Italiana di Microfinanza" Italy is one of the European countries with the highest financial exclusion, equal to approximately 25 % of the population, and microcredit reaches only 8000 people. The reality appears to be extremely fragmented and unable to cope with the fact that in Italy three million families don't have a checking account.

This fragmented situation makes any study dangerously uncertain. Too often operators differ in some part of their micro-credit project, or are too small to have a significant impact in the study that is unlikely to reveal whether microfinance can operate on a large scale in Italy.

One aspect that distinguishes the Italian operators than the Grameen Bank is that often the micro loan is made to the consumer to exit from emergency situations, like a big unexpected expense to pay. However, the client has to prove that it has a constant stream of income in order to bear the extra cost of the micro loan (in Italy, interest rates oscillate between 8-15%).

This factor automatically excludes the poor from access to this form of micro-credit. You could argue that trust is a cornerstone of the movement and that requiring a form of income is avoidable. Instead it is a matter of logic : if a person is poor, without any source of income, it is one thing to give him/her some money so you can find them invest and repay the debt, it is another to lend money that will not create any source of income and thus become a burden for the individual. Therefore we have to exclude microcredit for consumption for this definition of microcredit.

In Italy, also, the microloan is not as "micro" as the Grameen Bank's. The latter expects that with a loan of just € 30-100 you can change a person's life, and it could be repaid within a year of the emission.

How can a poor return, not 25000 €, but only 10,000 euro in a year? With an average rate of 10 % it would result in monthly instalments of just under 1000 Euros, a figure prohibitive even for people with a job. As a result, loans in Italy are diluted over the course of several years, this leads to a slow down of the climb up the social ladder as the person who received the loan is burdened with it for longer.

Another underrated aspect of the Grameen model is the weekly payment of installments. Unfortunately there isn't yet a reliable scientific study on the positive effects of this method, however, the experience in Bangladesh shows that this is one of the main reasons for the success of the Grameen -style microcredit.

One of the he reason behind it is that, since weekly installments are smaller than monthly ones, people find it easier to "break away" from the owed money as, apparently, it is easier to do so with smaller sums rather than larger ones. The fact that the person has to pay weekly makes this event an element of everyday life rather than an extraordinary one. In addition, it is easier for the banks to spot problems with the borrower, for example the bank will start to investigate after three missed repayments. In the case of monthly fees, much more time has to pass before the bank becomes aware of any situations affecting the borrower.

Another difference is that, within the Italian context, microcredit is strongly directed towards immigrants. In fact, due to the large increase of the phenomenon, more and more banks have turned their attention to microcredit projects just for this section of society.

Microcredit is therefore has become a feasible mechanism of social integration of these new people who are already in financial trouble and are likely to remain on the margins of society if nothing is done about it.

6.3 Statistics of micro-credit in Italy

According RITMI microloans disbursed in Italy have increased fivefold in the last 2 years. However, the Italian situation is very different from that of other European countries. In Italy, in fact, we observe a large number of micro-finance institutions (32 are actually counted but those estimated there are about 80) with a relatively low number of loans disbursed .

However, there has been a remarkable growth of the sector. A survey published in 2011 showed that in 2007 a total of 392 loans were made by 27 institutions. In 2009, the number of loans granted by 32 institutions have reached 2146, changing, in monetary terms, from € 3.634 million in 2007 to around € 12.74 million at the end of 2009 (Fourth Report on Microcredit in Italy , 2011).

Even after we factor in the increase in number of institutions , the rise in the number of loans turns out to still be very significant .

The beneficiaries of this growth of microcredit appear to be mainly women and immigrants.

However, we have to note that the statistical information from RITMI is not exhaustive as it has failed to provide a specific definition for micro credit meaning that it will lead to an inaccurate representation since microcredit is often confused with other microfinance projects .

In addition, the lack of specific legislation in Italy and measures to support the sector during the years of the study has hindered once again the accuracy of the information collected. This lack, however has been addressed in 2010 where through an ammendment to the "Testo Unico Bancario" (Consolidated Banking Act), a whole section (articles 111-113) has been dedicated to microcredit and regulation of operators specializing in microfinance.

6.4 The role of banks and institutions

Before describing the role of banks, institutions, foundations, and non-profit organizations in the provision of microcredit, it should be noted that the Italian situation is diverse and fragmented. In addition, Italy has a long tradition of lending to disadvantaged segments of the population. In Italy, there is often confusion between microcredit and microfinance, as some organizations perform both activities. At the structural level, the strategic modus operandi is also completely different from the Grameen Bank, which is much more attentive to the person rather than the guarantees that he or she offers. In addition, many of the bodies that provide microcredit are not born of banking origin; indeed, the influence of a banking drive and a centuries-old tradition of lending have significantly distorted Yunus's vision.

In Italy, the financial realities are different to what the Grameen Bank had to face; thus, the methods of providing microcredit are very different, especially if the initiatives are headed by traditional banks. The models of lending that are closer to the one developed by Yunus are used by non-profit organizations such as Caritas. Owing to their internal structures, these seem to be the ideal partners for the management of practical support and solidarity. Their proximity to the territories, the ubiquity of listening centers and the depth in the social fabric keep this organization in close contact with the community, and thus it takes the role of a social indicator of problems. The counseling centers become such efficient "agencies" that, besides the production of forms of material support for applicants (food parcels, generic services, medical care), they act as nuclei for the development of any active policies.

In the past years the increasingly strong appeal for help by the listening centers for the bands of populations which are financially less stable has sparked the first steps for programs of financial support including microcredit. The first step is to obtain cooperation from other institutions.

Once it has been decided on the issues that have to be addressed, Caritas, often through other asociations that represent it, start to tackle the problem with the formation of a guarantee fund, usually co-funded by local lenders, from local authorities (City and County) and the institutions of civil support (companies, co-operative sector, social associations, representative bodies). Microcredit is the final step of operating this route, and it is usually afforded to applicants through the identification and analysis of the sustainability of requests.

A technical selection committee (composed of members of the same Caritas, representatives of associations and local authorities, and also a figure linked to the lenders of the fund) checks the repayment plan and the feasibility of the operation, with the same Caritas who plays the role of ensuring the equity of the client. The request is then considered and scrutinized by lenders who support the initiative (in particular, Banca Etica, cooperative banks), and, if accepted, provide the microfinance (amounts ranging from 1000 to 25,000–30,000 euros, depending on the type of employment). The loan is repayable in monthly installments (usually between 1 and 3 years, with possible further scope for slight delays in the return of the sum lent), at a reduced rate that may be null or reduced compared with commercial rates.

The fund is of the rotary type: contributions are "shared" with additional responsibility if not returned within the terms and conditions agreed upon. The repayment of the loan allows the recovery of the sum and the further use for other requests (ZERBETTO, 2003). For the duration of the loan, the institution does not lose contact with the person concerned, but rather accompanies him with a series of advisory services and training, such as highlighting binding initiatives and identifying a sustainable design. This kind of free advice contributes to the enhancement of the contribution of the loan and produces positive effects in terms of return. In fact, know-how is a central presence not only in businesses, but also for use in the support of social projects.

The return process reaches higher levels as well. From a conceptual point of view, the micro-enterprise develops a two-dimensional application: one part emergency credit (with smaller loans - 1000/3000 Euro - and a reduced repayment period), and the other loans for micro-activities (ranging from 15,000 to 25,000 Euro).

6.4.1 PerMicro

One of the most important companies dedicated to microcredit in Italy is PerMicro, a company founded in Turin that operates throughout Italy and provides small loans. PerMicro identifies its customers among those with difficult access to the banking system and offers loans without requiring collateral. It was created to offer financial services on a fair and transparent basis in order to combat financial exclusion and provide support for individual and family development paths. The goal is to become a social business that offers these services without relying on external aid.

PerMicro has developed an alternative method to that of group lending to replace the collateral undrawn. The relationship between the applicant and the "bank" is tightened through a network, which carries out the role of moral guarantor. The networks most frequently used are the centers of aggregation as parishes or ethnic communities, or local associations and cooperatives.

The offering of PerMicro is characterized into two main types: microcredit for the enterprise and microcredit for the family. Microcredit for the enterprise is the main operational side of the company and this is aimed at individuals excluded from traditional credit. An important aspect is that it offers loans not only for starting a business but also for the development of micro-enterprises. The requirements for this type of access to microcredit are having a good business idea, having the ability to run your business and being part of a referral network that is willing to ensure you morally. In addition, the company is committed to providing support for other activities, such as the preparation of the business plan for the duration of the loan.

Microcredit for families, by contrast, aims to cope with the transitional needs of households or individuals. For valid reasons such as medical care, housework, training or the education of children, PerMicro offers loans of up to 15,000 euros with preventative advice to clarify the conditions. However, the differences with the Grameen microcredit model are many. Microloans for families are for consumption, women are not privileged, payment is in monthly installments rather than weekly, and the bank does not go to people but vice versa.

6.4.2 Mag2 Finance

Another institution dedicated to microcredit is Mag2 Finance, which is a cooperative of financial solidarity. Mag2 uses its capital to provide small loans to individuals, companies (cooperatives) and associations for entrepreneurial activities in Italy. Those excluded from the traditional banking system are taken into account. In this case, the differences with the Grameen Bank are enormous, too. For example, they fund companies, and therefore do not represent the poorest of the poor. further, they give loans for consumption and not just for micro-entrepreneurship and there is no strategy of empowerment for the poorest parts of the population.

6.4.3 Fondazione San Carlo

The foundation of San Carlo is a non-profit organization that deals with various themes and carries out several activities, including microcredit since 1999. This is carried out with the collaboration of Solidatas, Bocconi University and three banking groups, namely BPM, Deutsche Bank and Unicredit. The microcredit project is non-profit and consists of granting loans, up to a maximum of 7,500 euros, to the socially disadvantaged to start micro-enterprises or self-employed activities. The foundation guarantees support for the duration of the loan. Since 1999, it has funded 80 projects. This operator seems to be the most similar to the Grameen Bank, but you have to take into account the fact that it has promoted

80 projects in 11 years. It is too little to talk about the real functioning of microcredit because no data are available on the customers of these 80 projects.

6.4.4 Micro.Bo

Micro.Bo was founded to spread the knowledge and practice of microfinance in Bologna and its province. In addition to a dedicated staff, there is also support from volunteers. Micro.Bo believes that only through intervention and cooperation between public and private non-profit organizations is it possible to meet the multiple and interconnected needs expressed by stakeholders. It offers microcredit borrowers training and coaching for the wise management of the family budget, financial literacy, conservation educational and legislative assistance about the renegotiation of mortgages. It also plays an active role in research and experimentation and offers training on dissemination activities and information about microcredit. Micro.Bo also created emergency microcredit for people living in Bologna that may require a micro-loan in the event of problems (medical care, unforeseen expenses for real estate, purchasing basic equipment).

6.4.5 Compagnia di San Paolo

The Compagnia di San Paolo was born in Turin in 1563 as a charitable brotherhood and it is now one of the largest private foundations in Europe. The foundation participates pursues public interest and social utility in order to guarantee the civil, cultural and economic development of the communities in which it operates. Development is thus the goal and also the standard by which it evaluates its initiatives.

Its areas of intervention are manifold including scientific research, economic and legal, education, art, health and assistance to vulnerable social groups. The foundation's activities are funded with revenues generated by the assets gathered over the centuries, assets that the company has the duty to pass on intact to future generations. Among its many social innovation projects was the Microcredito della Compagnia di San Paolo (Microcredit of St. Paul's fellowship), which aims to facilitate banks granting loans in favor of people who have difficulties accessing credit in order to support economic development.

The main purpose of this project is to empower vulnerable social groups in order to reduce the obstacles in the system that make it difficult to access credit. In addition to overcoming this barrier, there are other equally important objectives: development of potential, the training and growth of the individual, education for the responsible management of savings, freedom from a logic welfarism and the prevention of situations of usury.

Entities applying for funding must be resident or established in the provinces of Genoa and Naples, the Lazio Region and within the territory of the Diocese of Turin, which covers most of the municipalities of the province of Turin and communes in the provinces of Asti and Cuneo. Further, they must also be individuals or individuals associated with each other in the form of partnerships, social cooperatives or a small cooperative society.

The minimum amount of funding available is €2,000 for the initiation and development of economic activities and €500 for projects related to employability; further, the maximum amount of funding is €20,000 for single persons and €35,000 in the case of partnerships, social cooperatives and small cooperative societies. In addition to cash loans, credit commitments, specifically bank guarantees, for a total amount not exceeding 10% of the total guaranteed funds may also be granted. Loans are returned in monthly installments (18–60 months with a possible grace period of six months).

6.4.6 Fondazione Giordano dell' Amore

The Foundation Giordano dell' Amore was incorporated under Italian law in 1977 by Cassa di Risparmio delle Provincie Lombardy and it thus has its own assets. It offers training, technical assistance and research in the areas of finance for banks, economic and financial ministries, and public and private organizations. The foundation is not for profit, and covers a proportion of its internal costs from the proceeds of its assets, while its actions are co-funded by other bodies. It is a center for the collection and exchange of knowledge on microfinance issues in Italy and in the world, offering its knowledge to organizations or countries that request it.

While the foundation does not mind lending or microcredit, microfinance is the center of interest. It carries out the functions of business, research, training and technical assistance regarding this issue. It has also received prizes for the best microcredit projects with the dual aim of publicizing the movement and giving further opportunities to develop the best projects.

6.4.7 Micro Progress Onlus

Micro Progress Onlus is a non-profit organization founded in Rome in 2004 to promote and implement projects of microcredit and microfinance both in Italy and abroad. The association was founded under the name of the Centro Studio per lo Sviluppo e la Cooperazione (Study Centre for Development and Cooperation). Its first target was intervening in developing countries and working at different stages of the microcredit projects: feasibility, management, monitoring and impact analysis.

However, during its first years of activity, Micro Progress Onlus began to consider the opportunity to put into practice what was learnt abroad in Italy. Moreover, even in other Western countries such as France, Britain and the United States, microfinance was becoming a central tool to fight poverty and support social and economic exclusion. For this reason, from 2006 Micro Progress Onlus decided to redefine its mission, while maintaining an interest in the activities of countries in the developing world, adding support to the attention of those who, in Italy, were excluded from the right to access credit.

No less important is its interest in facilitating socio-economic integration by contributing to the creation and intensification of interpersonal relationships based on trust and mutual commitment. Mainly, Progress Micro offers microcredit in Rome and its provinces, while providing technical assistance to microcredit projects in Italy and abroad. In Rome, it has launched a project called "not only consumer credit" with the help of PerMicro Spa. This proposes the same approach as microcredit a the guarantee of a social network that is committed to helping the customer in the case of problems. Like PerMicro, it requires that the client has an idea for a business or that a family needs small amounts.

6.4.8 Extrabanca

Extrabanca is a new independent bank that consists of 44 members, including the Fondazione Cariplo and Assicurazioni Generali. The main feature of this bank is that it relates primarily to foreign citizens in Italy. Among the many services offered, there is also microcredit. In this case, the service is called Extraprestito, and it has very similar characteristics to microcredit: the possibility to choose a total amount from 2500 to 30000 euros as well as to vary the duration from 24 to 84 months to obtain a lower rate. Extrabanca is the first Italian bank aimed primarily at foreign communities residing in Italy. It is not just a bank but also a company that offers a set of services with the aim of promoting economic development and the social integration of this part of the population that contributes more significantly to the growth of the country.

6.4.9 Banca Etica

Founded in 1999 by the activities and thrust of Mag2, this institute acts as a representative of the third sector and brings together organizations of the social world as well as financial support from thousands of adherents to civic citizenship. The organizational network of Banca Etica has a number of branches and financial advisors scattered all over the country, according to the concept of neighborhood, which is the heart of the ethical message that identifies customer centricity and contributes to the reduction of the costs of asymmetric information.

The bank aims to combine ethics and the operation of credit with the management of savings and generating value in a context of financial sustainability, attention to the practices of environmental protection and respect for civil society and the individual. In fact, it has ethical guidelines that support a clear vision for the operational management of enterprises, in which the rights of the person (to credit, participation, social cohesion and relations) are superimposed onto economic management and influence current operations.

Participation in activities by participants must also be proactive as well as economically and socio-culturally legitimate, which is why it promotes a policy of customer loyalty. According to the participative design promoted by Yunus, this involves a more heartfelt adherence to the values of transparency and solidarity, with a view to supporting and promoting the community.

In the given context, microcredit is developed according to the specific conditions identified. The use of microcredit is bidirectional; in fact, it is intended for both individuals who are not able to provide guarantees for business activities and individuals in need. Loan schemes vary from the creation and support of micro- and small businesses to planning distinctive core values regarding welfare. It thus outlines the construction of a partnership with strong local roots.

These operations often take place with logistical support by geopolitical structures, including the fundamental contribution of Caritas, a match in terms of the forms of gift (in the broad sense) and reciprocity of Christian values. From an operational point of view, the resources for microcredit are obtained through a fund that donates 1 euro for every 1000 euros collected. The projects considered are usually evaluated by mutual agreement through negotiations with the entity listening (Caritas), and then internally by an evaluation committee.

This bank, therefore, differs from the others in that it seeks to "inspire all its activities, both operational and cultural, based on the principles of Ethical Finance: transparency, rights of access to credit, efficiency and attention to the non-economic consequences of economic actions. The mission is to manage savings towards the socio-economic initiatives that pursue social goals and operating in full respect of human dignity and nature".

A bank that defines itself in this way could omit a microcredit project. In fact, Banca Etica uses microcredit to promote two main types of interventions: programs for the establishment or support of micro-enterprises and social welfare programs. The second project seeks to respond to needs in some fundamental aspects: expenditure must be temporary and unexpected and it must be incurred to meet a basic need. However, the subject must already have an income even though the spending needs to improve his situation. Even though the Ethical Bank prides itself on being committed to delivering micro-loans, the fact that it requires an income to access funds places it outside the model of Yunus.

6.4.10 Banca Prossima

Founded in 2002 by a joint initiative between Banca Intesa and San Paolo IMI, Banca Prossima is an institution for the third sector that offers loans for social activities, with a committee that checks the conditions of the validity of the loan (Solidarity Committee and Development). Its activities are better described as subsidized loans rather than microcredit, and aimed at social enterprises rather than individual figures. The loans are for a number of initiatives (prevention of usury, immigrant entrepreneurship, student loan) aimed at the social context (in this case, access to credit application sees a different approach from microcredit).

From an operational point of view, the bank offers access to credit for individuals traditionally close to the third sector and the implementation of projects and sustainable products according to a banking vision. Banca Prossima seems to be more linked to the expansion of the financial sector and compliance with standards of profitability and efficiency, rather than a design related to the concepts of ethical relevance. The rates applied and shape of the structure tend to develop projects with high economic returns, which seem to overlook the true value of microcredit.

BIBLIOGRAPHY

AA. VV. (2005), Povertà e vulnerabilità sociale: un percorso di ricerca in Studi Zancan-Politiche e Servizi alle Persone n. 3/2005

AA.VV., (2000), Vulnerabilità sociale e processi d'impoverimento in Sociologia Urbana e Rurale n. 62/2000

Abbink, K., Irlenbusch, B. e Renner, E. (2006) Group Size and Social Ties in Microfinance Institutions, in « Economic Inquiry », 44, n. 4, pp. 614-628.

Accorinti M. - Mirabile M. L. – Romano M. C. – Sgritta G. B. (1998), Profili di povertà estrema. Dieci anni di attività assistenziale della Caritas Diocesana di Roma in Assistenza Sociale n. 1/1998

Adams, J. e Raymond, F. (2008) Did Yunus deserve the Nobel Prize: Microfinance or Macrofarce?, in «Journal of Economic Issues», 42, n. 2, pp. 435-443.

Addabbo, T. (2000): "Poverty Dynamics: Analysis of Household Incomes in Italy", Labour, Vol. 14, No. 1, pp. 119-144.

Adelman L. – Middleton S. – Ashworth K. (2003), Britain's poorest children. Severe and persistent poverty and social exclusion, Save the Children London 2003

Agulnik, P. - Hills J. (2002), Understanding social exclusion, Oxford University Press Oxford 2002

Alcock P. - Siza R. (a cura di) La povertà oscillante in Sociologia e Politiche Socialn. 2/2003

Alcock P. (1997), Understanding Poverty, Macmillan London 1997

Alcock, P. (1999): "Understanding Poverty", seconda edizione, Macmillan Press, Londra.

Alesina, A. e Glaeser E.L. (2004) Fighting poverty in the US and Europe. A world of difference, Oxford-New York,

Alkire, S. (2002): "Dimension of Human Development", World Development, Vol. 30, No. 2, pp. 181-205.

Anand, S. (1977): "Aspects of poverty in Malaysia", Review of Income and Wealth, Vol. 23, pp. 1-16.

Anand, S. (1983): "Inequality and poverty in Malaysia. Measurement and Decomposition", Oxford University Press.

Anand, S. e A.K. Sen (1994): "Human Development Index: Methodology and Measurement", Occasional Papers, No. 12, Human Development Report Office.

ANDREANI E., (2003), *Il rapporto tra banche ed imprese in Germania*, in *Banca, impresa e società,* n. 3, 2003, pp. 321-353.

Antonelli G., (2005), *Dopo lo Tsunami. Sri Lanka: ricostruire la speranza,* in *Mondo possibile*, 2005, pp. 12-15.

Apospori E. - Millar, J. (2003), The dynamics of social exclusion in Europe, Edward Elgar Publishing Cheltenham 2003

Asselin, L. e A. Dauphin (2001): "Poverty Measurement: A Conceptual Framework", Canadian centre for international studies and cooperation, dal sito:
www.crefa.ecn.ulaval.ca/develop/Poverty.pdf.

Atkinson, A.B. (1970): "On the measurement of inequality", Journal of Economic Theory, Vol. 2, pp. 244-263.

Attanasso M.O., (2004) *Analyse des déterminants de la pauvreté monétaire des femmes chefs de ménage au Bénin »*, Mondes en Développement, Vol.32-2004/4-n°128, pp. 41-62

Avallone P., (a cura di), *Il "povero" va in banca. I Monti di Pietà negli antichi stati Italiani (secc. XV-XVIII)*, Napoli, 2001

BAGELLA M. (1999), *Proprietà e criteri di gestione delle Fondazioni bancarie: questioni in discussione* in *Sviluppo Economico*, vol. 3, n.2- 3, maggio - dicembre 1999.

BALDAN C., (2006), *Il capitale finanziario e il rapporto banca e industria,* Torino, 2006.

Baldan C., (2006), *Il capitale finanziario e il rapporto tra banca ed industria,* Torino, Giappichelli.

Barile N. L., (2010), *Credito, usura, prestito ad interesse*, in Reti medioevali, maggio 2010

Becchetti L., (2008), - Il microcredito: [una nuova frontiera per l'economia], Bologna, Il Mulino, 2008

Becchetti L., (2010), *Il microcredito: Una nuova frontiera per l'economia,* Il Mulino, Bologna,

Becchetti, L. E Castriota, S. (2011), "Does Microfinance Work as a Recovery Tool After Disasters? Evidence from the 2004 Tsunami", *World Development*, Vol. 39, No. 6, pp. 898-

Becchetti, L., Castriota, S. E Conzo, P. (2012), "Bank Strategies in Catastrophe Settings: Empirical Evidence and Policy Suggestions", CSEF Working Paper No. 324

BIANCO M., (2002), *L'industria italiana*, Bologna, il Mulino, 2002.

Bocchella N., (2007), *Il sistema del microcredito: teoria e pratica,* Ed. Lel, Milano.

Borgomeo C. et al., (2008), 4° Rapporto sul microcredito in Italia, Catanzaro, Rubettino.

Borgoneo C., (a cura di), (2012) Dimensioni e prospettive del prestito sociale e imprenditoriale in Italia, Donzelli editore.

Bruni L., Crivelli L., (2004), Per una economia di comunione: un approccio multidisciplinare, Roma, Città Nuova Editrice.

CAPRIGLIONE F., (1988), *Costituzione di banche e rapporto banca-industria,* in scritti in onore di M.S. Giannini, vol. III, Milano, 1988

Caruso E., (2003), L'impresa in un mercato che cambia. Modelli e strumenti di gestione, Milano, Tecniche Nuove.

Chabot I., Fornasari M., (1997), *L'economia della carità. Le doti del Monte di Pietà di Bologna (secoli XVI-XX)*, Bologna, 1997

Corigliano R., (2007), *Banca e impresa in Italia: caratteri evolutivi del relationship lending e sostegno dello sviluppo* in *Banca, Impresa e società,* n. 1, Aprile, 2007, pp. 34.

Daley-Harrys S., (2009) State of the Microcredit Summit Campaign Report 2009, Washington, DC, Microcredit Summit Campaign, 2009.

Fanfani T., (a cura di), (2003), *Alle origini della Banca. Etica e Sviluppo economico*, Roma, 2003

Gentilini A. M., (1995) Il leone e il cacciatore, storia dell'Africa sub sahariana, La Nuova Italia Scientifica, Roma, pp.389-402

Giordano F., (2007), *Storia del sistema bancario italiano*, Donzelli editore, Milano, 2007.

Giovannini R., (2013) Bastano 100 super-ricchi per sconfiggere la povertà nel mondo, La Stampa, 21 gennaio 2013.

Gonzalez A., Narain S., Rosenberg R., (2009) The New Moneylenders: Are the Poor Being Exploited by High Microcredit Interest Rates? , Consultative Group to Assist the Poor, <http://www.cgap.org/gm/document 1.9.9534/OP15.pdf> .

Gonzalez A., Narain S., Rosenberg R., (2009) Are Microcredit Interest Rates Excessive?, Consultative Group to Assist the Poor, <http://www.cgap.org/gm/document1.9.9536/BR_Are_Microcredit_Interest_Rates_Excessive.pdf> .

Hossain M, (1988), Credit for alleviation of rural poverty: The Grameen Bank in Bangladesh, IFPRI - International Food Policy Research Institute, (in collaborazione con BIDS – Bangladesh Institute of Development Studies), Research Report n. 65, Febbraio 1988.

Kraemer H., Conforti A., (2009), Microfinance in Europe: a market overview, Luxembourg, European Investment Fund.

Latifee H.I., (2009) The Future of Microfinance: Visioning the Who, What, When, Where, Why, and How of Microfinance Expansion Over the Next 10 Years, Bangladesh, Grameen Trust, 2009.

LIMENTANI R. (2006), *L'evoluzione del rapporto banca – impresa: dalla Hausbank al financial services advisor,* in *Banca, impresa e società*, n.1, 2003.

M. Yunus, (2010), *Un mondo senza povertà*, Milano, Universale Economica Feltrinelli, 2010.

Manservisi L., (2013), *L'usura si nasconde anche in banca e gli istituti rimborsano i clienti,* in *ravenna e dintori,* 2 giugno 2013.

Masciandaro D., Riolo F., (a cura di), (1997), *Crisi d'impresa e risanamento: ruolo delle banche e prospettive di riforma,* Milano, 1997

Meneghin V., (1986), *I Monti di Pietà in Italia dal 1462 al 1562*, Vicenza, 1986

Merusi F., (1982), *Opera pia e impresa bancaria nelle Casse di Risparmio***,** in Studi Tosato, Milano 1982

Miglietta G., (2004), *Esperienze di microcredito della Caritas Italiana a livello internazionale* Caritas Italiana - Seminario di studio "Il microcredito: uno strumento internazionale di lotta alla povertà" – Roma, 17-18 marzo 2004.

Muzzarelli M. G., (2001), *Il denaro e la salvezza. L'invenzione del Monte di Pietà*, Bologna.

Nardone, A. e Villa A. (2008), *La realtà del microcredito in Europa*, in Corsi, M. (a cura di), *Donne e microfinanza*, Aracne editrice, Milano.

Niccoli A., Presbitero A.F., (2010) *Microcredito e macrosperanze: opportunità, limiti e responsabilità,* Egea, Milano,.

Nowak M., (2005), (traduzione di Mario Marchetti) - Non si presta solo ai ricchi: la rivoluzione del

Nowak M., (2005), *Non si presta solo ai ricchi, La rivoluzione del microcredito,* Enaudi, Torino.

Onetti A., Pisoni A., (2005), *Le relazioni tra industria e finanza in Germania all'inizio del terzo millennio: una mappa interpretativa,* Quaderni dell'Università di Insubria, Settembre 2005.

Paugam S., (1996), *L'exclusion, l'état des savoirs* (sous la dir. de), Paris, La Découverte, coll. « Textes à l'appui »,

Paugam S., (1999), *L'Europe face à la pauvreté. Les expériences nationales de revenu minimum garanti*, (sous la dir. de), Paris, La Documentation Française, coll. « Travail et Emploi », 1999.

Paugam S., (2002), *La société française et ses pauvres. L'expérience du revenu minimum d'insertion*, Paris, Presses Universitaires de France, coll. « recherches politiques », 1993, 2ème édition mise à jour 1995, coll. « Quadrige » 2002 (avec une nouvelle préface à l'édition « Quadrige »).

Paugam S., (2003), *La disqualification sociale. Essai sur la nouvelle pauvreté*, Paris, Presses Universitaires de France, coll. « sociologies », 1991, 4ème édition mise à jour 1997, dernière édition dans la coll. « Quadrige » 2009 (avec une nouvelle préface "La disqualification sociale vingt ans après") (traduit en portugais, Sao Paulo, Educ/Cortez et Porto, Porto Editora, 2003).

Paugam S., (2007), *Le salarié de la précarité. Les nouvelles formes de l'intégration professionnelle*, Paris, Presses Universitaires de France, coll. « Le lien Social », Série « Documents d'enquête », 2000, coll. « Quadrige » 2007 (avec une nouvelle préface à l'édition « Quadrige »).

Paugam S., (2007), *Repenser la solidarité. L'apport des sciences sociales* (sous la dir. de), Paris, PUF, coll. « Le lien social », 2007.

Paugam S., (2008), *Le lien social*, Paris, PUF, coll. « Que sais-je ?»,

Paugam S., (2008), *La pratique de la sociologie*, PUF, coll. "L.

Paugam S., (2008), *La régulation des pauvres* (avec Nicolas Duvoux), PUF, coll "Quadrige".

Paugam S., (2010), *L'enquête sociologique* (sous la dir.), Paris, PUF, coll. « Quadrige », 2010.

Paugam S., (2010), *Les 100 mots de la sociologie* (sous la dir.), Paris, PUF, coll. "Que sais-je ?", 2010.

Paugam S.,(2005), *Les formes élémentaires de la pauvreté*, Paris, Presses Universitaires de France, coll. « Le lien social », 2005, traduit en espagnol (Alianza Editorial, 2007), en allemand (Hamburger Édition, 2008).

Pelgreffi P., (2009), Il microcredito: una risposta ai problemi delle famiglie e delle microimprese, per emancipare dal bisogno, promuovere autonomia, generare responsabilità sociale, Fondazione G. Dalle Fabbriche

Prahalad C.K., (2007) The Fortune at the Bottom of the Pyramid. Eradicating Poverty through profits, Upper Saddle River, N.J., Wharton School Publishing-Pearson Education, 2006 (La fortuna alla base della piramide, Bologna, Il Mulino, 2007).

Ragazzini G., Ragazzini M. (1995), Breve storia dell'usura, Clueb, Milano, 1995.

Salsa E., (2005), *Il sistema produttivo e il rapporto banca – impresa*, San Paolo IMI, Torino, 2005,

Sen (1985): "Commodities and Capabilities", Professor Dr. P. Hennipman lectures in economics: Vol. 7, Elsevier Science Publishers, Amsterdam.

Sen, A.K. (1976): "Poverty: an ordinal approach to measurement", Econometrica, Vol. 44, No. 2, pp. 219-221.

Sen, A.K. (1979): "Issue in the measurement of poverty", Scandinavian Journal of Economics, pp. 285-307.

Sen, A.K. (1980): "Equality of What?", in Sen (1982), pp. 353-369.

Sen, A.K. (1981): "Family and Food: Sex bias in Poverty", in Sen (1994), pp. 346- 368.

Sen, A.K. (1982): "Choice, Welfare and Measurement", Basil Blackwell Publisher, Oxford.

Sen, A.K. (1983a): "Development: which way now?", The Economic Journal, Vol. 93, pp. 745-762.

Sen, A.K. (1983b): "Poor, relatively speaking", Oxford Economic Papers, 35, pp. 153-169.

Sen, A.K. (1983c): "Rights and Capability", in Sen (1984), pp. 307-324.

Sen, A.K. (1984): "Resources, values and development", Basil Blackwell Publisher, Oxford.

Sen, A.K. (1992): "Inequality Reexamined", Oxford University Press, Oxford.

Sen, A.K. (1993): "Capability and Well-Being", in Nussbaum e Sen (eds) (1993), pp. 30-53.

Sen, A.K. (1994): "Well-being, Capability and Public Policy", Giornale degli Economisti e Annali di Economia, Vol. 53 (nuova serie), No. 7-9, pp. 333-348.

Sen, A.K. (1997a): "La libertà individuale come impegno sociale", traduzione di C. Scarpa, editori Laterza

Sen, A.K. (1997b): "On Economic Inequality", Clarendon Press, Oxford.

Sen, A.K. (1999): "Development as Freedom", Oxford University Press, Oxford.

Sen, A.K. (2000): "Social Justice and the distribution of income", Handbook of Income distribution, Vol. 1, pagg 59-85.

Stiglitz J.E., (2006) Microfinance and Missing Markets, New York, Columbia University,

Surowiecki J., (2008) What microloans miss, The New Yorker, finanziaria del 17/03/2008

Tarantola A.M. (2007), *Banche e imprese: opportunità e sfide alla luce di Basilea II,* in *Rivista Bancaria,* n. 6, nov. Dic., 2007.

Teichner A., (2009), Il pricing nel microcredito, Università La Sapienza di Roma – Associazione Docenti Economia Intermediari Mercati Finanziari (ADEIMF).

The Economist (2007); *Briefing: Sri Lanka - A war strange as fiction, The Economist,* June 9th 2007, pp.23-26.

Tramonto E., (2008) Microfinanza per i paesi ricchi, uno strumento utile ma anche un business, in "Valori", n. 57, Marzo 2008, pp. 6-8.

Welfare Regimes and the Experience of Unemployment in Europe (avec Duncan Gallie, sous la dir. de), Oxford, Oxford University Press, 2000.

World Bank, (1995), Khandker S.R., Khalily B., Khan Z., *Grameen Bank: Performance and Sustainability,* World Bank Discussion Papers; n. 306, Ottobre 1995.

Yunus M., (2006) Discorso pronunciato dal premio Nobel per la Pace del 2006 Muhammad Yunus in occasione della premiazione, Stoccolma, The Nobel Foundation.

Yunus M., (2010) *Un mondo senza povertà,* Milano, Universale Economica Feltrinelli, 2010.

Yunus M., (2006), Il banchiere dei poveri, Milano, Feltrinelli.

Yunus M., (2007) Vers un monde sans pauvreté, Paris, Jean-Claude Lattès, 1997, (Il banchiere dei poveri, Milano, Universale Economica Feltrinelli,.

Yunus M., (2010), Vers un nouveau capitalisme, Paris, Jean-Claude Lattés, 2008, Un mondo senza povertà, Milano, Universale Economica Feltrinelli, 2010.

Yunus M., *What is microcredit?, (*2010*)* Grameen Bank, luglio 2010, <http://www.grameeninfo. org/index.php?option=com_content&task=view&id=28&Itemi d=108>.

Zamagni, V. (2000), (a cura di) - Povertà e innovazioni istituzionali in Italia: dal Medioevo ad oggi, Il Mulino, Bologna, 2000.

Zerbetto, C., (2003), Banchieri ambulanti: presente e futuro nella finanza etica e nel microcredito - Cooperativa Editoriale Valori, 2003.

Copyright © 2013 by Edoardo Bonacina

All rights reserved. This book or any portion thereof may not be reproduced or used in any manner whatsoever without the express written permission of the publisher except for the use of brief quotations in a book review or scholarly journal.

First Printing: 2013

ISBN 978-1-291-68401-8

Piazza Stefano Jacini
Rome, Lazio 00191